NIDDERDA

'Flow, lovely Nidd, along thy winding bed,
By towering firs and stately oaks o'erspread!'

To the River Nidd
Thomas Blackah of Greenhow Hill

Nidderdale

A David Leather

Smith
Settle

First published in 1995 by
Smith Settle Ltd
Ilkley Road
Otley
Wset Yorkshire
LS21 3JP

ISBN   1 85825 042 0

British Library Cataloguing-in-Publication data:
A catalogue record for this book is available
from the British Library.

Set in Monotype Ehrhardt

Designed, printed and bound by
SMITH SETTLE
Ilkley Road, Otley, West Yorkshire LS21 3JP

For John and Christine Rose.

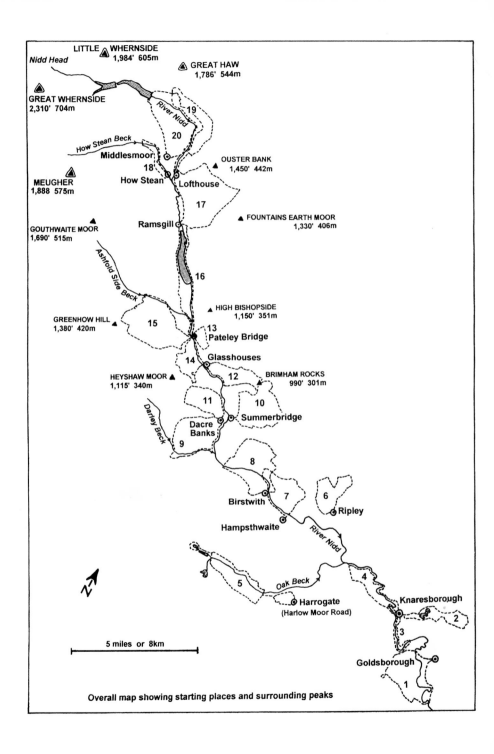

LITTLE WHERNSIDE
1,984' 605m

Nidd Head

GREAT HAW
1,786' 544m

GREAT WHERNSIDE
2,310' 704m

River Nidd

19

How Stean Beck

20

Middlesmoor

OUSTER BANK
1,450' 442m

18'

MEUGHER
1,888 575m

How Stean   Lofthouse

17

FOUNTAINS EARTH MOOR
1,330' 406m

GOUTHWAITE MOOR
1,690' 515m

Ramsgill

Ashfold Side Beck

16

HIGH BISHOPSIDE
1,150' 351m

GREENHOW HILL
1,380' 420m

15

13

Pateley Bridge

14   Glasshouses

HEYSHAW MOOR
1,115' 340m

12

BRIMHAM ROCKS
990' 301m

11

10

Darley Beck

Dacre
Banks

Summerbridge

9

8

7

6

Birstwith

Ripley

Hampsthwaite

River Nidd

N

5

Oak Beck

4

Knaresborough

Harrogate
(Harlow Moor Road)

2

3

5 miles or 8km

Goldsborough

1

Overall map showing starting places and surrounding peaks

CONTENTS

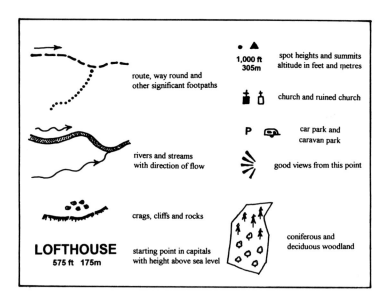

route, way round and
other significant footpaths

spot heights and summits
altitude in feet and metres

1,000 ft
305m

church and ruined church

rivers and streams
with direction of flow

P   car park and
caravan park

good views from this point

crags, cliffs and rocks

coniferous and
deciduous woodland

LOFTHOUSE

575 ft   175m

starting point in capitals
with height above sea level

INTRODUCTION

As Nidderdale possesses its own fine landscape of unspoilt beauty, it had every right to be part of the Yorkshire Dales National Park when it was formed in 1954. The reason it was excluded was connected to the fact that the head of the dale formed extensive gathering grounds for Bradford's water supply. In those days, access to areas where clean, fresh water was being collected was strictly limited as far as the public were concerned, and there was a restriction, too, on new building. By keeping people out, the water could be kept reasonably pure and uncontaminated.

However, in more recent years, the purity of drinking water is dealt with after it leaves the reservoirs, and this has led to more freedom of movement in the catchment area. The reservoirs of Gouthwaite, Scar House and Angram have now become part of Nidderdale's landscape. They enhance the otherwise bleak moorland surroundings and are appreciated by visitors for peaceful walking and recreation in a scenic environment, little changed since the last reservoir was finished in 1936.

In the spring of 1994 the whole of Nidderdale as far down as Birstwith, just above Harrogate, became part of an Area of Outstanding Natural Beauty. It is a fitting tribute to the dale, which will now receive protection from haphazard development. The new AONB also includes Fountains Abbey and Colsterdale to the north and the Washburn Valley to the south.

This *Walker's Guide* contains twenty fine walks, carefully chosen to take in as many interesting points and historic places as possible. They range from three to nearly twelve miles (5 to 19km) and average about seven (11km). There is a good network of footpaths in the dale, though many are as yet not signposted or waymarked. However, those along the Nidderdale Way are generally well signed. The centre for the upper dale is Pateley Bridge, which makes an excellent base for the walker as so many good walks are within easy reach. Lower down the dale just below Ripley, the river enters an attractive, deep, wooded gorge, only emerging from it some six miles (10km) further on at Grimbald Bridge, below Knaresborough.

A visit to the historic town of Knaresborough (population, 14,000) is a 'must', as there is so much to see, and some splendid walks along the river and in the countryside about. Harrogate (population 64,000) is also within the drainage area of the Nidd, and there is a fine walk from the town centre that visits Harlow Carr, Havarah Park and Beaver Dyke reservoirs. Below Knaresborough the valley opens out, and the guide includes another six miles of the meandering River Nidd as far as Little Ribston, with a walk from Goldsborough to include Plumpton Rocks.

Suggested times are for walking only. Allow for stopping to look around, catching your breath, taking photographs and for picnics. The maps are large and easy to follow. The starting point is named in large capitals and heights above sea level are given, both for the start and often for the highest point on the walk. I have tried to keep north at the top of the page, but this is not always possible. For a broader view of the area, the Landranger maps 99 (Northallerton and Ripon) and 104 (Leeds, Bradford and Harrogate) cover all of the walks.

Small changes to routes of footpaths take place from time to time as footpaths evolve, but these are usually well signposted. There is likely to be a change in the area of Plumpton Hall at some stage *(walk 1)* and possibly at Dinmore House *(walk 7)*. New rights of way now include the circuit of Angram Reservoir and the ridge from Dead Man's Hill to Little Whernside. Some tracks are not marked as rights of way on the map, but come under the heading of 'unclassified county highways'. Tracks on Fountains Earth Moor are in this category. Occasionally, far from anywhere, you meet another walker who goes by without a word, but most people say hello, so do pass the time of day. You may even strike up an interesting conversation, meet someone you know or make new friends.

My thanks are due especially to Douglas and Olwen Middleton, and also Joyce Hartley, Ken Limb and Philip Rack for their local and specialist knowledge, to the Footpath Officer for the Nidderdale area, and local residents who have been so helpful; also to Hilary Roper for the lovely watercolours and drawings; to John Edenbrow, Trevor Croucher, Peter Smith and C R Kilvington for some of the colour photographs; and to Trevor Croucher for the cover photograph. Thanks go, too, to Mark Whitley and Smith Settle for their patience and guidance in the preparation of this guide.

When you are out for a walk in Nidderdale, please leave the wild flowers, rocks and fossils undisturbed for others to enjoy, and take back only happy memories, photographs, notes or sketches. Respect the people who live and work in the countryside, and remember the Country Code.

ACKNOWLEDGEMENTS

Thanks are due to the following people for permission to reproduce the undermentioned illustrations:

Trevor Croucher, cover, p122.
John Edenbrow, pp6, 41, 54, 85.
C R Kilvington, p40.
Douglas and Olwen Middleton, pp3, 26, 28, 100.
Hilary Roper, pp15, 16, 17, 19, 21, 24, 25, 27, 35, 37, 46, 66, 74, 80, 83, 97, 106, 110, 123.
Peter Smith, pp30, 51, 84, 95.

All maps, diagrams and other illustrations were provided by the author.

PUBLIC TRANSPORT

Rail services: Trains run regularly between Leeds and York, stopping at Harrogate and Knaresborough.

The **Dalesbus** network includes a regular two-hourly bus service (No 24) each day (except Sundays) from Harrogate to Pateley Bridge. The *Dales Connections* public transport guide is free from National Park centres or (enclosing a 9"x 6" SAE) from Elm Tree Press, The Elms, Exelby, Bedale, North Yorkshire, DL8 2HD.

Nidderdale Rambler: A Sunday and Bank Holiday park-and-ride bus service from Harrogate (Victoria Avenue) operates from April to September, calling at Killinghall, Hampsthwaite, Birstwith, Darley, Dacre, Dacre Banks, Summerbridge, Brimham Rocks, Smelthouses, Wilsill, Glasshouses, Pateley Bridge, Wath Land End, Gouthwaite Reservoir, Ramsgill, Lofthouse and How Stean Gorge. The service (no 24) runs both in the morning and afternoon, and is operated by Harrogate and District Travel. Timetable leaflets may be obtained from Harrogate Council, Department of Technical Services, Knapping Mount, West Grove Road, Harrogate. Explorer tickets may be used on this bus (available on the bus).

TOURIST INFORMATION CENTRES

Royal Baths Assembly Rooms, Crescent Road, **Harrogate**   (01423 525666)
Market Place, **Knaresborough**   (01423 866886)
High Street, **Pateley Bridge**   (01423 711147)

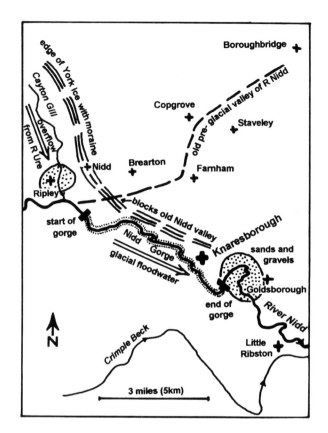

The origin of the Nidd Gorge. The old course of the Nidd became blocked by the York ice-sheet, and water flowed south to cut a new channel (the Nidd Gorge). Water from the Ure Valley (also blocked) poured down Cayton Gill, adding to the size of the Nidd. Both Ripley and Goldsborough are on or near gravel patches deposited by the floodwater. (See page seven for a fuller description.)

ROCKS AND THE LANDSCAPE

Nidderdale has more than its fair share of beautiful, unspoilt countryside, and indeed is one of the most interesting of the Yorkshire dales, largely because of its rich history. Although not part of the National Park, it has recently been designated an 'Area of Outstanding Natural Beauty'. Squeezed between the larger valleys of Wensleydale and Wharfedale, the vale of the Nidd pushes out beyond the edge of the Pennines and into the Vale of York, and is different in many respects from the other dales.

There is less limestone, a rock that often adds interest to local scenery, though where it does show up it produces some remarkable natural features like How Stean Gorge and Goyden Pot, near Lofthouse. However, most of the dale is dominated by the overlying millstone grit and, not to be outdone, the gritstone outshines itself in the spectacular formations of Brimham, Guisecliff and Plumpton Rocks. Further down the valley, at Knaresborough, are outcrops of the softer, buff-coloured magnesian limestone.

There are three large lakes in the dale, and the lack of limestone has been an advantage for the siting of these reservoirs, as well as for the provision of soft water. They have certainly transformed the scenery of the upper dale and, until more recent times, a need to keep the water pure meant limiting new building and also restricting access to the public. So the unspoilt and tranquil nature of this area is due in part to the extensive gathering grounds of Bradford waterworks.

An unusual feature of Nidderdale is that the dale is not a through route to anywhere. For the motorist, there is an escape route over to Masham and the lower part of Wensleydale, but only walkers can exit from the head of the dale either by ancient routes over to Coverdale or on to Starbotton or Kettlewell in Wharfedale.

The River Nidd   The infant stream begins at Nidd Head Spring, not far from the summit of Great Whernside (2,310 feet, 704m) and, after a steep drop, it enters the large reservoirs, first of Angram, and then Scar House. Further along it reaches limestone and disappears underground for a distance of two miles (3km), to reappear in copious springs just below Lofthouse. Soon after the village of Ramsgill it is 'lost' again in the waters of Gouthwaite Reservoir, an important nature reserve.

Between Pateley Bridge and Ripley, the river curves round to the east again as it skirts the foot of Brimham Moor; then, near the hamlet of Nidd, it enters the Nidd Gorge, a steep-sided glacial overflow channel. Warm spa water is added by tributary streams from the Harrogate area, and the Nidd makes its picturesque way through Knaresborough, still deep in its gorge, before finally breaking out onto the plain near Goldsborough. The river finally joins the Ouse some fifty miles (80km) from Great Whernside at Nun Monkton just above York.

Geology of the Dale

Carboniferous limestone   This is the oldest rock and occurs in four small but influential patches, two in the upper dale near Lofthouse, one on Greenhow Hill and the other near Harrogate.

The young River Nidd, after leaving Scar House Reservoir and taking a bend to the south, entirely disappears into its own bed where it meets limestone. Both

1

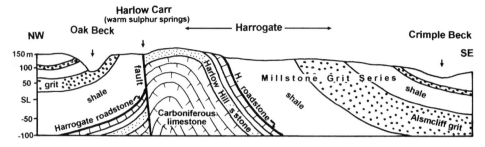

NW Harlow Carr (warm sulphur springs) Oak Beck ← Harrogate → Crimple Beck

The Harrogate Anticline, which brings carboniferous limestone to the surface, as well as the many spa water springs for which the town is famous. Length of the section three miles (5½km).

Manchester Hole and Goyden Pot *(walk 19)* are in this section and, in normal conditions, those who care to explore the entrance of either of these caves will hear the roar of the river on its subterranean way through a complex system of passages. Even after heavy rain Manchester Hole will swallow most of the water but, occasionally, floodwater will reach Goyden Pot along the surface, though this cave is rarely completely flooded. The limestone around and in the entrance to Goyden is rich in fossil corals and brachiopods. The large lamp-shell *Gigantoproductus* is well seen in section on the boulders, looking like white crescent moons — of the two shells that enclosed the animal, one is concave and the other convex. The dissolving effect of water on the limestone is well displayed in the entrance passage, where its surface is glazed and scalloped. The stream bed below Goyden Pot is covered with grass where gritstone outcrops at the surface. Both the river and its limestone passage are completely hidden below the gritstone. The river appears again near Lofthouse, at Nidd Heads, just below the road *(walk 17)*.

A second patch of limestone outcrops along the floor of How Stean Beck *(walk 18)*, as well as along a short stretch of the Nidd near to Lofthouse where it is cut off to the south by the Lofthouse Fault. At the

famous How Stean Gorge, the beck has cut a narrow canyon deep into the limestone (to a maximum of eighty feet, or 24m), producing impressive miniature limestone scenery. The effect of swirling water is seen in the rounded undercutting of the sides of the ravine and in the circular potholing of the streambed. The path follows the rim of the gorge along limestone ledges, in one place below an overhang so that you have to bend down as you walk; in another you can scramble down to water level. The beck can be a peaceful stream or a wild torrent depending on the weather. At the upper end of the gorge an underground stream emerges from How Stean Tunnel, and on the north bank is the entrance to Tom Taylor's Cave, through which it is possible to walk (with the use of a torch) the 200 yards (180m) to an exit in the café car park at Cat Hole.

The limestone at Harrogate *(walk 5)* is brought to the surface by an upfold in the strata known as the Harrogate Anticline *(see cross-section above)*. It is along the centre of this fold that the many springs of spa water occur, for which the town is famous. The springs contain a proportion of salt and sulphur with iron in varying amounts. They are unusual in that they arise along geological faults, especially one that runs parallel to the crest of the fold, where the main

2

springs of Harlow Carr, Bogs Field and the Pump Room occur. The flow of water is very slow — only a few gallons per hour — in contrast to springs fed by rainwater which may yield thousands of gallons per hour. Some of the springs are warm, about 54°F (12°C), so they must be from deep below ground, and the saltiness of the water suggests that it could actually be 'fossil' sea water from ancient Carboniferous seas, long trapped in the strata. Such brines are capable of carrying metals such as lead and zinc in the form of sulphides, and may have deposited the galena of the leadmines higher up the dale.

Reminders of the past in rocks from Scotgate Ash Quarry, near Pateley Bridge: (above) fossil worm casts; and (below) ripple marks caused by strong currents in prehistoric shallow seas.

Greenhow Hill *(walk 15)* has limestone coming to the surface also in an anticline, part of the same system of folds that include the Skipton, Skyreholme and Harrogate anticlines. Today there is a very large limestone quarry on the crest of the hill, largely worked for aggregates and road metal. However, in the past, Greenhow was an important leadmining area, the whole hillside being riddled with mines and passages. Mining is known to have begun 2,000 years ago as ingots of lead, weighing 155 lbs (70kg), have been found bearing Roman inscriptions, like the one in Ripley Castle *(walk 6)*. Most of the mining was carried on from the seventeenth to the nineteenth centuries along the Garnet and Sun veins, with further activity in Ashfold Side to the north as mining followed the rich Providence and Merryfield veins. Common minerals include galena (PbS), fluorite (CaF_2), barite or barytes ($BaSO_4$), sphalerite (ZnS) and calcite ($CaCO_3$).

Millstone Grit   Most of the scenery of Nidderdale from Great Whernside to Knaresborough is in millstone grit, and reflects the more or less horizontal beds of sandstone that alternate with shales. The original sands and muds were laid down some 320 million years ago in a huge delta that covered much of the area of northern England and was deposited by rivers bringing debris from northern mountains.

The present-day scenery is a sombre moorland, where broad stretches of heather and cotton-grass grow in the peaty, acid soils. Some of the gritstone bands (gritstone is a coarse sandstone) are particularly thick, and form the rugged crags and cliffs of Yeadon (above Wath), Guisecliff and Brimham. The softer shales are rarely seen and form lower-lying ground.

Brimham Rocks, high on the east side of Nidderdale, form one of the most dramatic gritstone outcrops in the country. They consist of a number of large stacks of rock, many of which are undercut and

3

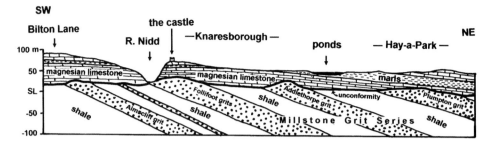

A section across the River Nidd at Knaresborough shows how the magnesian limestone lies on the eroded millstone grit series. The gritstone formed hills in a desert landscape, which the Permian sea gradually covered, depositing the limestone. The unconformity is the junction between the two ages of strata — the thick line. Length of section 4 miles (6½km).

weathered into grotesque and strange shapes, scattered over fifty acres (20ha) or so of Brimham Moor. The rocky edge of the moor is visible from miles away, but most of the shaped rocks can only be seen from close by *(walks 10 and 12)*. They have been a tourist attraction for 200 years, and many have kept their names of Dancing Bear, Druid's Writing Desk, Lover's Leap, Mushroom, Turtle, Camel and so on.

Their formation, in the Kinderscout Grit, has been due to the presence of strong joints between the stacks, along which weathering and erosion have taken place, leaving one lot of rocks separate from another. Undercutting may be partly due to wind erosion, especially during a post-glacial dry period, though that part of the rock nearest the ground remains damper longer, and this may also speed up weathering in that zone. Layers of 'softer' rock where, for example, there are finer bedding structures or less cement between the sand grains, are also more easily eroded, so that you get the effect of a pile of rocks, one stacked upon another. On Fountains Earth Moor *(walk 17)*, rocks known as Jenny Twigg and her Daughter Tib have been left standing isolated among the heather.

Plumpton Rocks, south of Knaresborough, are made of the same Kinderscout

Grit and make up another outstanding formation *(walk 1)*. Large amounts of building stone have been quarried in upper Nidderdale, and the stone industry is described in the next chapter.

Magnesian Limestone Knaresborough is built on a 'bluff', or cliff, of magnesian limestone. This pale yellow rock of Permian age (younger than the Carboniferous) sits directly on millstone grit *(see cross-section above)*. It was about this time (about 270 million years ago) that the Pennine block was uplifted, the anticlines created and, in this district, all of the coal measures eroded away, as they appeared above sea level. Most of the British area became dry land, where hot desert conditions prevailed (New Red Sandstone times) and, in Yorkshire, an arm of the sea reached the new Pennine shore.

Along Waterside by the river *(walk 3)*, the boundary between the millstone grit and the overlying magnesian limestone forms a classic example of an unconformity. This means that the strata above do not lie parallel to the rocks below (they do not 'conform') and implies a gap in time in the order of millions of years. In this case the whole of the Coal Measures is missing, having been eroded away, before the limestone was deposited. The unconformity itself is

The cliffs along Waterside, Knaresborough, showing the unconformity of magnesian limestone on millstone grit. (The contact point is halfway up the lamp-post.) Before the limestone was laid down, the whole of the coal measure strata had been deposited on top of the millstone grit and, in this area, eroded away again. The junction between the two rock types — the unconformity — represents a gap in time of about sixty million years.

5

At How Stean Gorge near the head of Nidderdale, How Stean Beck has cut a narrow canyon up to eighty feet (24m) deep into the limestone, one of the few outcrops of that rock in the dale.

irregular, indicating that the old gritstone surface had been worn into humps and hollows before the deposition of the limestone. The hollows contain reddish desert sand followed by 200 feet (60m) of limestone.

The limestone is different from that of the upper Dales because it contains not just calcium carbonate, but also a proportion of magnesium (in the form of the mineral dolomite), a sign that the seawater was drying up under the hot sun and becoming more and more salty. Fossils are rare and show stunted growth. The present-day scenery on the limestone is not very distinctive, but the soils are basic and support a wide variety of flowering plants.

6

Plumpton Rocks offer a fascinating and wonderful display of rock formations, the millstone grit naturally sculptured by erosion into fascinating shapes. The rocks and the nearby lake are also a valuable sanctuary for birds.

The Ice Age and the Nidd Gorge During the last part of the Ice Age, Nidderdale's own glacier had its beginnings on the slopes of Great and Little Whernside. In the upper dale it gouged out a classic glacial trough and, as the ice retreated, mounds of rubble and clay in the form of terminal moraines were deposited across the valley at Gouthwaite, Pateley, Glasshouses and Darley. Use was made of the moraine at Gouthwaite for the siting of the dam, and

that at Glasshouses helps hold up the mill dam there. Lower down the valley, sheets of boulder clay, some three to twelve feet (1 to 4m) thick, cover most of the underlying rocks.

About 20,000 years ago a large ice sheet was moving down the Vale of York, blocking the natural course of the rivers Ure, Nidd and Wharfe. Meltwater, released in the warmer summers, was ponded up against the ice in a vast lake, which then overflowed south. The River Ure flowed down Cayton Gill *(walk 6)*, depositing the gravel patch on which Ripley stands. The primeval River Nidd was diverted along the line of the present Nidd Gorge *(walk 4)* as it made for the Crimple Valley. Here, the torrents of water continued to cut deeply into the boulder clay and into solid rock. This 'overflow channel' became so deep that the Nidd never went back to its former bed, which was choked by a large moraine that had built up along the edge of the York ice. The old pre-glacial channel of the Nidd can be traced from Ripley, between Scotton and Brearton, through Farnham and Copgrove towards Boroughbridge *(see map on opening page)*.

At the lower end of the Nidd Gorge, all the vast amount of debris eroded from the gorge came to rest in a broad gravel fan, near to the village of Goldsborough *(walk 1)*. As the ice melted, so vegetation began to cover the land once again. Birch and alder grew to the tops of the present moors, while on the lower slopes were dense oak woods, with alder and willow in the valley bottoms. As man came on the scene, the natural order changed again.

7

MAN AND THE LANDSCAPE

Early man Nidderdale has the earliest signs of man in the Dales. In the 1920s, Major E R Collins discovered implements, made of local chert, of late Upper Palaeolithic period (Old Stone Age). The people were cave dwellers who lived at the end of the Ice Age, between 12,000 and 8,000 BC, and had entered Britain on foot, before the formation of the English Channel. A large hand-axe and several scrapers were found near Goyden Pot, and others near Angram and Scar House reservoirs. Neolithic (New Stone Age) axes have been found on Pateley Moor and at Birstwith, and a Bronze Age axe was discovered on Heathfield Moor, near Pateley Bridge.

These early people were hunters and pastoralists, and had little effect on the landscape. It was not until the Celtic (Iron Age) people arrived in the third century BC that people made clearings in the woodland for more permanent settlements. The Celts or Ancient Britons — the large Brigantes tribe who occupied this area — had a good system of farming and used small hand grindstones, known as querns. The name of Whernside is actually 'quern-side', a probable source of supply of the stone. Two other British names are Nidd, meaning 'brilliant', and Dacre, 'trickling stream'.

The Romans The main Roman influence in the dale was the working of leadmines in the Greenhow district, above Pateley Bridge. Three Roman pigs of lead have been found in the area, one of them now lost. The other two were found together in a hole on Heyshaw Bank in 1737. Inscriptions on the base refer to 'Emperor Domitian's seventh term as consul', this being the year AD 81. The letters BRIG, marked on the side, are thought to be short for Brigantes, the people who were forced to work in the mines. One of the bars of lead can be seen in Ripley Castle *(walk 6)*. The Roman road from Ilkley to Aldborough crossed the Nidd near Hampsthwaite and then to Ripley.

Angles and Norsemen The Angles, or English, came into Yorkshire from what is now northern Germany in the sixth and seventh centuries. They were mainly arable farmers who established village communities in lower parts of Nidderdale. Place names are a good guide to their distribution, with *-ley* (clearing) and *-ton* (farm or village) being the most common of the early names. Ripley is thought to come from the Hrype tribe, who founded Ripon, and could be the first English settlement in the dale. Other *-ley* names of clearings along the valley include Bewerley, Darley, Pateley, Whipley and Winsley, while among the *-tons* are Cayton, Brearton, Scotton, Plumpton and Ribston.

After some Danish settlement in the ninth century, mainly in the lowland areas (Clint is a Danish name), the tenth century saw a movement into the upper dale of Norsemen from the north-west, having come via Ireland and the Lake District. The farms were spread out, and name elements of *-gill*, *-beck* and *-thwaite* date from this time, in places such as Armathwaite, Gouthwaite, Thornthwaite, Ramsgill, Raygill and Fell Beck.

The Norman Conquest After the Northumbrian rebellion of 1069, Yorkshire was more or less devastated by William the Conqueror. People were killed, houses burned, and crops and cattle destroyed. By the time of the *Domesday* survey, seventeen years later, all fourteen places listed in

8

A relic of medieval piety is the Chapel of our Lady of the Crag, a wayside shrine cut in the cliff at Knaresborough by John the Mason in about 1408. The figure guarding the entrance is likely to be a Knight Templar, one of an international religious-military order who were involved in the Crusades.

Nidderdale, except one, were described as waste.

Monastic times   Soon upper Nidderdale was acquired by the two Cistercian abbeys of Fountains and Byland. Fountains established some thirty lodges and granges between Ripley and Lofthouse; while on the east side of the upper dale, in the townships of Stonebeck Up and Stonebeck Down, Byland had nineteen. (The granges were farms run by lay monks.) The small 'monks' chapel' at Bewerley was built about the year 1500 for the tenants of the large grange there, and has been beautifully restored *(walk 14)*. Stretches of 'monk wall', marked on Ordnance Survey maps, indicate the extent of the boundary of abbey lands, which on the south side bordered on Knaresborough Forest.

Much of the south side of Nidderdale and the lower dale came under the Crown as part of the great Forest of Knaresborough, the two deer parks of Haya and Havarah being created as game reserves. 'Forest' was an administrative term, meaning a hunting area, though there was a fair amount of woodland within it, particularly on less fertile ground and steep valley sides. At one time the tree-cover must have been extensive, as it was said that a squirrel could pass from Padside Hall to Ripley Castle without once touching the ground, a distance of eight miles (13km).

People within the Forest lived in hamlets and villages surrounded by meadows. They had certain rights, and were allowed to collect peat and firewood, and timber for building repairs, but there were restrictions on grazing and the taking of green

9

branches; and dogs had to have clipped claws. King John, who stayed at Knaresborough Castle on several occasions, went hunting here in 1210 and 1211; and in 1355, Edward III, while hunting in Knaresborough Forest, was saved from an enraged wild boar by Thomas Ingilby — the first of a long line of Ingilbys of Ripley — whom the king promptly knighted. On his tomb in Ripley Church, the head of Sir Thomas rests on a wild boar.

The fourteenth century was a catalogue of disasters. In 1314-15, bad weather prevented the harvesting of crops and there was famine. In 1318, invading Scots burned 140 houses in Knaresborough as well as the parish church and most of the granges up the dale. As if that wasn't bad enough, two years later cattle plague infected the area and few animals survived. Things gradually improved but in 1349 came the Black Death. Carried by fleas that lived on the black rat, it killed almost fifty per cent of the people of Nidderdale, including whole families. In 1361, a further outbreak became known as 'the plague of the children', the young being less immune to the disease, and another bad outbreak occurred in 1369.

The end of a way of life came with the dissolution of the monasteries in 1539, when the treasures and lands of Fountains and Byland abbeys went to the king. The Yorke family bought land in the upper dale that belonged to Byland Abbey, and the Ingilbys extended their land to include Dacre, Bewerley and Hartwith. These two families remained firmly Catholic and had fines levied against them from time to time. During the Civil War, the Ingilbys supported the king and, on 2nd July 1644, at the fateful Battle of Marston Moor, they found themselves on the losing side. That night, the victorious Cromwell and his men rested at Ripley Castle. It is said that Lady Ingilby faced Cromwell with two revolvers in case he made trouble. By December, Knaresborough, too, went to the Parliamentarians, and after that the castle was largely dismantled.

Farmhouses and walls The seventeenth century saw a prospering of yeoman farmers, who built fine stone farmhouses and halls ('the great rebuilding'), replacing the normal thatched cottage. Look out for the lintel over the door that may carry the initials of the people who first lived there, together with the date. For example: Dacre Low Hall, 1635-MW; a farm at Darley, 1667-WL EL; Dowgill Farm, Hartwith, 1679-RMO; and Bouthwaite Grange, 1673-RI. Some large landowners

Brimham Lodge, one of thirty such lodges founded in the dale by Fountains Abbey, was rebuilt in 1661 by Thomas Braithwaite; today it is an impressive farmhouse, with the base of an ancient sundial stood outside.

The graceful arch of the beautifully-built packhorse bridge that crosses the Nidd at Birstwith in a single seventy foot (21m) span. There was a timber bridge here in the sixteenth century, and it was part of the network of packhorse routes along which goods were transported. The present bridge was built in 1822 and became known as New Bridge. It is still only a footbridge, being just 6 feet (1.8m) wide.

rented their farms on 3,000 year leases which gave the same kind of security as outright purchase. Thwaite House was built in 1742 on the site of a grange, and to escape the window tax had two windows blocked out and others labelled 'cheese room' and 'dairy' so that they would be exempt.

Well-run farms, able to breed cattle and sheep, needed walled fields and the enclosure of land gradually increased. Most of the wall building took place in the late eighteenth century. According to a survey of 1794, Nidderdale was by then entirely enclosed, with small stone-walled fields, the farmers often combining butter and ham production with work in flax and lead-mining. Some of the moorland pastures were named after women such as Katty White and Jenny Twigg. For the poor farmer, enclosures meant the loss of common land and pasture for their animals, resulting in poverty or a complete move to industry.

Roads, tracks and turnpikes   In medieval times, Nidderdale had a network of monastic tracks. Routes from Fountains and Kirkby Malzeard crossed the upper dale on their way into Wharfedale and Calderdale, and another went from Lofthouse over to Jervaulx Abbey, while the many granges were linked along the valley.

As roads came to be used more frequently, by packhorses, wheeled carts and even coaches, their condition deteriorated so badly that in winter they became almost impassable. Turnpike roads were to solve

The smelt mill and shaft of Prosperous leadmine, at Ashfold Side near Pateley Bridge, which has been worked for hundreds of years. The mine still has a large cog-wheel jutting out of the top of it, and a collapsed flue runs up the hill slope.

the problem. They were planned by local landowners, merchants and traders, built with a hard surface and a toll was levied. However, road construction was still very basic and in need of some technical advance. And this is where John Metcalfe comes in, commonly known as Blind Jack of Knaresborough.

Blind from the age of four, this colourful character soon became a local guide, carrier, fishmonger and musician. He would play his violin for spa visitors, particularly at the Royal Oak Hotel in Harrogate. Here he fell in love with Dorothy Benson, the landlord's daughter and, it is said, eloped with her on the eve of her wedding to somebody else, marrying her himself the following day. It wasn't until the late 1760s, when he was forty-eight, that he became the leading road engineer in the north of England and a true pioneer, along with the great names of Macadam and Telford.

He built hundreds of miles of roads across northern counties, including bridges. The road between Harrogate and Knaresborough was over such boggy ground he 'floated' it on countless bundles of heather. In Nidderdale, he built the turnpike from Pateley Bridge to Grassington. (The other two turnpike roads from Pateley Bridge, one to Ripley and the other to Knaresborough, were built by the contractor John Smith.) The wheeled instrument Blind Jack used for measuring distances, his viameter, is on display in Knaresborough's museum. This remarkable man was happily married for forty years and lived to be ninety-two. He died in 1810 in Spofforth, where his gravestone records his eventful life in verse.

Lead, flax and stone industries   Most of the leadmines in the dale were concentrated in a small area near Pateley Bridge, at Greenhow and along Ashfoldside Beck. Old workings long deserted, some Roman and some medieval, were referred to as 't'owd man', conjuring up the picture of a bearded old miner of a bygone age. Rich veins were reached by long adits or tunnels driven into the valley sides, vertical shafts on the hill being for ventilation or access. When the ore was brought from the mine, it came to the surface mixed together with waste limestone and white minerals, such as calcite and barite. To distinguish the two white minerals, weigh them in your hand. The heavy one is barite, nearly twice the density of calcite.

'Dressing' the ore separated the galena from the worthless rock, and involved crushing and washing it through a sieve. This took place near the mine entrance, and a lot of finely-broken debris can still be seen, for example, at Prosperous Mine (*walk 15*), where also there are the remains of a smelt mill. Another mill at Merryfield is a short distance upstream, and Providence mill is sited nearer to Greenhow on Brandstone Beck.

Smelting involved roasting the ore in a furnace, to drive off the sulphur. A long chimney up the hillside not only helped obtain a good draught but some of the metal condensed with the sulphur on the inside of it, later to be scraped off by child labour. A large smelt mill, owned by John Yorke, was built at Heathfield and served all the Yorke mines, including those at Appletreewick in Wharfedale, and was in use well into the twentieth century.

Flax was grown locally and, because of the advantage of soft water for steeping the fibres, Nidderdale came to specialise in the linen trade. By the end of the eighteenth century, the existing cottage industry gradually became mechanised when mills took over the weaving and then the spinning processes. Twenty-five looms were established in Knaresborough, which became noted for its high-quality linen. George and Elizabeth Metcalfe of Pateley Bridge set up a flax-dressing and spinning business. As new flax-spinning machinery was developed in the 1790s, mills began to appear at Dacre Banks and Smelthouses. At Shaw Mills in 1812, the Metcalfes opened their flax-spinning mill, and twenty years later they moved to Glasshouses. During this period, four flax mills were working near Knaresborough. Most of the

Goldsborough Hall, an impressive Elizabethan mansion built by Richard Hutton after the original hall was destroyed in 1587. In the 1920s it was the home of the Princess Royal and Lord Lascelles (later Lord Harewood), and Queen Mary was a regular visitor. It is now a home for the elderly.

13

Nidderdale mills rode out the depression of 1837-44 and the trade picked up. Castle Mill, the old linen mill by the river below Knaresborough Castle, produced such fine quality linen it was appointed manufacturer to the royal household and advertised 'Knaresborough Linens, now used in all the royal palaces'. Decline in the industry came around 1880.

In modern times, flax-growing is having a comeback as, east of Knaresborough, fields of pale blue are replacing those of yellow rape. But this time the plant is used for its seeds, for linseed oil, rather than its fibre.

The third big employer, especially in the upper dale, was the stone industry. Querns, millstones, flagstones, roofing slates and general building stone have long been an important natural resource over a long period, and 200 quarry sites have been documented in upper Nidderdale. It was the railway, which reached Pateley Bridge in 1862, that really benefited quarrying on a large scale, and resulted in the export of large quantities of building stone. This came at a time when leadmining was on the decline.

George Metcalfe had supported the building of a railway for many years and, adding to his brewing and flax concerns, developed Scotgate Ash stone quarries, just above the town of Pateley Bridge. He had a railway incline built, with a maximum gradient of one in three, for the 1,000 yard (915m) descent from the quarry to the railway terminus *(walk 13)*. By the turn of the century, fifteen large quarries and twenty smaller ones were operating in furious competition near Pateley. A decline started about 1905, but trade was revitalised, particularly as far as employment was concerned, by Bradford Corporation's building of Angram Dam. Another impetus was given in the 1920s during the building of Scar House Dam.

Most Nidderdale buildings are built of local stone, though the medium-grained sandstone from Scotgate Ash was found to be of a very high quality, and could be quarried and transported in substantial blocks. Apart from buildings in Pateley Bridge itself, this stone was used in building the National Gallery and the museums at South Kensington, and York Art Gallery, and large slabs were in demand for quaysides, railway platforms and steps to public buildings. The only working quarry in the dale today is Coldstones Quarry at Greenhow *(walk 15)*, where limestone is obtained for road aggregate. Many of the old quarries are now long grown over, no longer scars in the landscape but havens for wildlife.

The spa waters of Harrogate While out riding in 1571, William Slingsby, of Bilton Hall near Knaresborough, discovered a spring that tasted like the water he had drunk at the original town of Spa, in what is now Belgium. The spring was named Tewit Well and found to be chalybeate, iron being the main constituent. Today the well, under its dome on pillars, may be visited on the Stray. In 1631, another similar well was discovered half a mile (1km) away, becoming known as the Sweet Spaw, since it was reasonably palatable. The first public bathing house was built next to it in about 1663. Soon the sulphur well or 'Stinking Spaw' in Low Harrogate began to gain a reputation for its medicinal qualities, as visitors arrived to cure their ailments. Inns and lodging houses sprang up and, by 1700, Harrogate spa was established. The town and its reputation grew, and the coming of the railway in the mid-nineteenth century allowed the town to expand rapidly, when people were able to travel easily from London and other cities so that each summer there was a great influx of visitors. The Royal Pump Room, built in 1842, now houses a museum that tells the history of the spa.

Nidderdale's reservoirs Bradford's rapid growth during the nineteenth century led to further expansion of its water supplies. Gouthwaite was built to act as a compensation reservoir, storing plentiful water during the winter and releasing it during the drier summer to maintain an even flow in the river. Angram is the highest reservoir and was completed in 1914, and Scar House was ready by 1936. At the time it was built it was thought to be the largest masonry dam in Europe, measuring 170 feet (52m) high and 600 yards (550m) long. Scar House Dam employed 700 men, and made use of thirteen locomotives and twenty-five cranes. The pipeline to Bradford tunnelled four miles under Greenhow Hill. The light railway from Pateley Bridge took passengers as far as Lofthouse, and further opened up the dale in this direction.

Many of the field stiles in Nidderdale are of fine construction, with steps leading up to two stout stone uprights built into the wall, making a handsome squeeze-through type. There are several like this in the neighbourhood of Middlesmoor.

Tourism Nidderdale as far down as Birstwith, just five miles short of Harrogate, together with Colsterdale to the north and the Washburn Valley to the south, have been given the status of an Area of Outstanding Natural Beauty (AONB) and will now receive added protection when there are pressures of development. Gouthwaite Reservoir is a nature reserve of great ornithological interest. The beauty spots of How Stean Gorge and Brimham Rocks are the most visited scenic attractions, but one of the attractions for walkers is the peace and quiet, especially of the upper dale. The Nidderdale Way is a well-established, long-distance footpath between Hampsthwaite and Scar House, with loops which can be covered in day outings. Fishing is carried on along the whole length of the river, with fly-fishing for trout and grayling as far as the Nidd Gorge, below which there is a mixture of trout and coarse fishing. Canoeing takes place on the Nidd at Pateley Bridge, and rock climbing at Brimham and Guisecliff. The contrasting towns of Harrogate and Knaresborough are both tourist attractions in their own right, with plenty of interest for visitors. Harrogate, an upstart of the nineteenth century, has a wide variety of shops, a professional theatre, parks and gardens; while Knaresborough, with 1,000 years of colourful history, has its castle, market, parish church and riverside.

WILDLIFE

Some of the placenames on local maps are reminders of what wildlife there used to be in the district. Wild boar feature at Low Boar Hole and High Boar Hole *(walk 5)*, while deer must have roamed near Deer Buck Crags *(walk 9)*. The corncrake was last seen in 1984 in Nidderdale *(walk 2)* but once must have been common in Crake Lane (Darley). Ravens are now unlikely to be seen at Raven's Nest, though foxes must still frequent Fox Crags *(both in Ravens Gill, walk 14)*, while sparrowhawks at Sparrow Hawk Farm *(walk 13)* and ducks in Duck Street *(walk 15)* are certainly still with us.

Ramblers have the advantage of seeing the countryside at close quarters. You can see more if you stop for a few minutes. From a well-chosen picnic spot, you may see some interesting bird behaviour. Have a pair of binoculars handy, as you never know what you might see. Other groups of

The peacock butterfly is common throughout the dale. Emerging in April and May, they lay eggs on nettles and have a second brood in the autumn.

A goldfinch, a bird which prefers rough ground or gardens where plants are allowed to seed, perches on a clump of teasel and sea holly. It is the only bird able to extract the nutritious seeds from the teasel.

animals to look out for are insects, fish, amphibians, reptiles and a variety of mammals. To see an adder warming itself in the March sunshine, a dragonfly emerging from its old 'skin' or a water vole swimming in the river may be rare experiences, but such sights make a walk even more memorable.

Birds

Birdwatching is a major attraction in the Nidd Valley, where a mixture of moorland, rough hillside, woodland, stretches of open water and low cropland all provide a rich variety of habitats. The Victorian geologist Joseph Lucas, in his *Studies of Nidderdale* (1872), mentions seeing the nightjar and corn bunting, both now lost to the area. But since those days the valley has acquired several large reservoirs as well as flooded gravel pits, and both have attracted many new species, especially waterfowl and waders, and rare migrants are also to be seen.

Open water *(walks 1, 2, 5, 16 and 20)* Gouthwaite is the largest of the reservoirs, and is well-known across the north of England for birdwatching. Being shallow at the northern end, expanses of mudflats become uncovered in the summer and autumn months, when they attract feeding waders such as curlew, lapwing and dunlin, and reeds provide cover for many nesting birds.

Among the waterfowl, winter surveys at Gouthwaite include hundreds of mallard and teal, and large numbers of Canada geese, wigeon and goosander. Goldeneye, a boldly-pied sea duck, is also a regular winter visitor to Gouthwaite. Teal, the smallest of the ducks, gather in the autumn and winter in large numbers on exposed mud and in the adjoining shallow water. Their flight is often low and fast, and a close

view shows the male to have a handsome chestnut and green head.

Wigeon is another dabbling duck and a regular winter visitor, coming in from Siberia in the autumn. The male is distinguished by its grey body and chestnut head with a cream 'bald' patch on the forehead. The goosander, a sawbill duck with a long thin beak, has increased dramatically over the last twenty years. Odd pairs now breed on the Nidd and winter flocks congregate on several of the reservoirs.

Breeding birds at Gouthwaite include tufted duck, a diving duck with a drooping crest, the male having black and white sides. Another is the shoveler, a heavy-looking dabbling duck with a huge flattened bill, the male having a green head and orange patch on its side. Common sandpiper, ringed plover and little ringed plover nest on pebbly gravel. Also attracted are rare migrants such as ruff, sanderling and curlew sandpiper; and enthusiastic birdwatchers are always on the look-out for birds of prey such as osprey, which make occasional visits, goshawk, winter sightings of which are increasing, and even golden eagle, recorded very occasionally.

Scar House *(walk 20)* and Angram, Ten Acre, Scargill, Beaver Dyke and John O' Gaunt's *(walk 5)* are other reservoir refuges for water birds.

The former gravel pits to the north of Knaresborough *(walk 2)* are now valuable breeding places for many species. Smaller lakes include those at Plumpton *(walk 1)* and Ripley Castle *(walk 6)*, while several new wildlife ponds like those at Ribston Hall *(walk 1)* and Park House near Brimham have been constructed specifically to help conserve wildlife.

Rivers and streams *(walks 3, 4, 7, 9, 12, 14, 16, 18 and 20)* Along the Nidd and side-streams, the dipper and grey wagtail are closely associated with fast-flowing

Tufted ducks nest on many stretches of water throughout Nidderdale. It is a neat-looking diving duck, the male being black with a white side-patch, and a wisp of a crest.

water, joined by the common sandpiper in the summer. Keep a sharp look-out for the brightly-coloured kingfisher, too, as it flies low and straight to a new perch. Mallard, tufted duck and moorhen also inhabit the Nidd, though the moorhen has declined in numbers recently, apparently with the spread of mink. Heron will fish not just along the river but in the smallest of side streams. Most of the riverbanks are tree-lined, and summer visiting woodland birds such as the blackcap, spotted flycatcher,

redstart and willow warbler all frequent this type of habitat. At most times of year, the greater spotted woodpecker, four species of tit, and sparrowhawk inhabit the riverside.

Uplands *(walks 5, 9, 10, 11, 12, 14, 15, 17, 19 and 20)* The flanks of the upper dale rise through rough grassland to broad tracts of heather and cotton-grass higher up. Some of the best grouse moors are close to upper Nidderdale, where red grouse stay throughout the year, except in the worst

19

winters. By the end of March, curlew and golden plover return to find nest sites, and small numbers of merlin breed on the grouse moors. On bracken-covered slopes, whinchat may be seen perching on a prominent stem to deliver a scolding *tic-tic-tic* or a sweet chattery song, while two other summer visitors, the wheatear and ring ouzel, prefer rocky outcrops. The cuckoo is often heard along the moor edges, where it lays eggs in meadow pipits' nests. Skylarks, though less numerous than they once were, still pour out their endless song and, also heard on the wing, are the drumming snipe, the throbbing sound produced by vibrations of the outer tail feathers. Occasionally you may see a buzzard circling high in the sky, or perhaps a short-eared owl hunting close to the ground in a wavering flight.

Woods *(walks 4, 6, 7, 10, 11, 14 and 18)* Woodland offers so much cover for birds that it is easier to identify them by their song. Resident songsters include the blackbird, song thrush, chaffinch, wren and robin, and with a trained ear you might distinguish the great tit, blue tit and coal tit. If you start listening for birdsong in February, you can pick them up one at a time, starting with the robin. Soon others will chime in and, by March and April, the summer migrants arrive, adding to and complicating the general chorus. The chiffchaff is one of the easiest to learn — mainly a simple tip-tap imitation of its name. The willow warbler is so common that it gives you a good chance to become familiar with its rippling song of descending notes. The blackcap's song is a beautiful and varied warble, while the wood warbler's accelerates into a shivering *shreeeee* like a bouncing table-tennis ball.

In the woods in winter, there is a better chance of seeing birds through the bare branches, and you may be rewarded by catching sight of parties of thrushes, tits or finches in their search for seeds or insects. Chaffinches are joined by redpolls and siskins, and small birds like the long-tailed tit are more noticeable among the leafless trees, where they are accompanied by other tits and goldcrests as they move through the wood. The greater- and lesser-spotted woodpeckers are both resident throughout the year in the woods of the Nidd Gorge, together with the nuthatch and tree creeper.

Farms and farmland *(walks 1, 2, 5, 6, 8, 9, 15 and 16)* Lapwings make use of sheltered fields in the upper dale, as well as the freshly-ploughed land of the lowland, or waste corners by gravel pits or sewage farms. They like to have patches of bare ground or short vegetation nearby for feeding where, in spring, you may see them in a tumbling display flight. In the lowland below Knaresborough *(walks 1 and 2)*, the yellowhammer is a resident farmland bird, where it will take up a perch in a tree along the hedgerows to deliver its song of high notes ending in a drawn-out *chweee* ('little-bit-of-bread-and-no-cheese'). The linnet, a small finch with a pointed bill, is seen along the hedgerows and bushy corners of fields. In summer the male has a red breast and forehead. The song is an attractive musical twitter. Two other finches, often seen near to farms and villages where there are a few trees, are greenfinch and goldfinch. The greenfinch is thick-set with a stout bill, being greenish-brown with a yellow-green rump. The dainty goldfinch (with pointed bill) is a very handsome bird with a red, white and black head, and yellow wing-bar.

Swallows and house martins return to establish their nest sites each year after an incredible journey from southern Africa. Both build nests of mud plastered onto walls of buildings. Swallows build a simple cup and prefer inside walls of barns, sheds and porches, whereas the house martin's

The brown trout is very common all the way along the River Nidd.

nest is an elaborate structure with a narrow entrance on the outside of buildings. Pied wagtails are also attracted by the insects around farmyards, and these essentially British birds stay with us throughout the year, feeding alongside streams and ponds in winter.

Other Wildlife

Fish The Nidd is well-known for its brown trout. This is the most common and widely-distributed of all fish and lives naturally, not only in the river but in the reservoirs and even in the smallest headwater streams. Below Gouthwaite, rainbow trout are regularly introduced, and both like clean water with a gravelly bottom. The related grayling likes the fast-flowing clear stretches and successfully competes with trout.

Lower down in the middle reaches, particularly below Knaresborough, coarse fish such as chub, dace, barbel and roach tend to take over. The common chub is carnivorous, feeds on smaller fish and often rises for a fly. The lively dace, like the chub, prefers fast-moving water but moves around in shoals. In deeper pools as well as in swift currents, the powerful barbel may grow to eight pounds (3½kg) or more. The eel-like river lamprey is not a true fish but occasionally may be seen in the spring in the

21

gravelly stretches. It is a blood-sucker, up to twenty inches (50cm) long, spends some of its life at sea and will cling to a trout or salmon for a free ride back to the river. The presence of crayfish in the Nidd is also a good indicator of water purity. These lobster-like creatures live under stones near the edge of the river. Our native crayfish are under threat from a disease carried by an introduced American species.

Mammals Rabbits are all too common along the edges of woodland, where there are adjacent fields of pasture, and higher up the dale right to the moorland fringes, among bracken. Stoats live in hedges and woods, and often may be seen hunting a small rabbit, or even tackling a fully-grown one. They can be recognised by the orange-brown fur and cream fronts. The brown hare is quite common on the lower parts of the moors and in poorer pastures where clumps of reeds grow *(Havarah Park, walk 5)*. In woodland areas you are likely to see grey squirrels and you may also get a sighting of the shy roe deer. A herd of fallow deer is kept at Ripley Castle *(walk 6)*, but wild ones are occasionally seen in the woods of the Nidd Gorge *(walk 4)*.

The Otters and Rivers Project has surveyed Nidderdale for otters, identifying possible habitats and preparing for the encouragement of the return of this attractive and rare animal.

Another rarity is the pine marten, which could also return to the dale as its distribution widens. One was trapped in Wath Woods in 1860, and the geologist Joseph Lucas saw one on Ash Head Moor, above Lofthouse in 1880 — local names for it were fomard and sweet mart. This large and handsome relative of the stoat measures twenty-seven inches long (68cm) including a nine inch (34cm) tail, likes remote woodland and is nocturnal.

The Harrogate Naturalists have, over several years, carried out surveys on many of the smaller mammals. Of the insectivorous ones, the mole and hedgehog have proved to be the most widespread, and the three shrews (common, pigmy and water shrew) are more thinly distributed and rarely seen. Among the small rodents, the bank vole, field vole and wood mouse are the most common, but the distribution of these shy animals is only determined by use of Longworth traps, which allow them to be caught, identified and set free again.

Butterflies The small tortoiseshell and the peacock emerge in April and May. They lay eggs on nettles and have a second brood in the autumn. Both are widespread through the area. The red admiral is often seen with them, but rarely hibernates successfully, and most of those we see in May and June are migrants from the Continent.

In May the green hairstreak appears in sheltered hollows on the moors where bilberry grows, for example, on the slopes up to Greenhow *(walk 15)*. These tiny insects chase each other about in the sunshine to land on a stem and show off the bright green underside of their wings. Also in May, lower down the slopes *(walk 10)*, look out for the holly blue. This bright blue butterfly has spread rapidly over the last fifteen years in the middle part of the dale and is seen flying around holly trees. The female lays its eggs on holly flower buds, but for the second brood in the autumn, she lays them on ivy. So both holly and ivy are necessary for this insect to survive. Another blue butterfly, if seen in June or July, is likely to be the common blue.

In lowland parts, meadow brown and wall butterflies are common in the summer months; and in the same area, among elm trees, you may be lucky enough to see a white letter hairstreak, another butterfly that was formerly absent from the area and is now establishing itself.

FLORA

Nidderdale has less limestone, more standing water and reaches out further into the lowland of the plain of York than the other dales, and the slight differences in drainage, soils and rainfall are reflected in the flora. There are certain plants that make Nidderdale different.

As early as February, the dale provides a scattering of snowdrops. These beautiful delicate blooms will push through a covering of snow and make a spectacular show around villages and under trees. A real speciality of the dale is musk, *Mimulus moscatus*, a relative of the monkey flower. This unusual plant has small yellow flowers with a lush green foliage that is sticky and hairy all over. It is found in wet places and tends to lie back as if it is falling over. In spring, lower down the dale in woods and banks on the magnesian limestone, as on Grimbald Crag *(walk 1)*, you may come across a display of sweet violets, many of them white with perhaps a few purple ones dotted among them. The sweet violet is not so different from the common dog violet that grows more widely, but if there are white blooms among them, and of course if they are scented, then these are the sweet variety. An uncommon plant for the north of England is white bryony that climbs over the lowland hedges. The hanging clusters of green flowers develop red poisonous berries in the autumn.

Acid moorland *(walks 10, 12, 17, 19 and 20)*   Although Nidderdale has more reservoirs and lakes than the other dales, the rainfall on the eastern slopes of the

Every spring, bluebells carpet the floor of Cayton Gill Woods near Ripley.

23

The sweet violet tends to grow in woods and along riverbanks in the lower dale. It is similar in appearance to the common dog violet, which is more widespread.

Pennines is not so heavy. The acid moors of the upper dale are also fairly well-drained, so there is a wider covering of heather. Around the head of the dale are some of the best grouse moors in the country which, in August, turn to carpets of delicate purple. After shooting has finished in late October or early November, fine days are used to burn strips of heather, called swiddening, which encourages succulent young shoots, the food of the red grouse, the following spring. Near rocks or on short slopes, bilberry forms green patches, and where there are no sheep, as on Brimham Moor *(walks 10 and 12)*, bilberries and their fruit are at their best.

Other moorland plants in the area include cowberry (shiny green leaves and red berries), crowberry (a sprawling plant with black berries), cloudberry (a creeping member of the bramble family with large white flowers and orange fruits), cross-leaved heath (in wet places) and bell heather (on drier parts).

Carboniferous limestone *(walks 5, 15, 18 and 19)* Where there is limestone, like the small outcrops in the valley bottom above Lofthouse and at How Stean, there is always a greater variety of wild flowers, even though many are not expressly lime-loving. In the wooded gorge at How Stean *(walk 17)* grow herb robert, herb bennet, dog's mercury, wild garlic, germander speedwell, large bittercress, common forget-me-not and red campion.

An area of exposed limestone moorland at Greenhow *(walk 15)*, designated a Site of Special Scientific Interest or SSSI, has some unexpected delights, such as the many cowslips that grow near the water tower; and, on the south side of Coldstones Quarry, there is an abundance of scurvy-grass, mountain pansy, harebell, spring sandwort and wild thyme. Scurvygrass is a member of the cabbage family and, although it commonly grows near the coast, is also found in the Dales. The high content of vitamin C made it a good cure for scurvy, a disease which often afflicted sailors who were at sea for long periods. Mountain pansy, usually a beautiful yellow, grows near limestone and seems to survive even in the most exposed sites. Spring sandwort is a small, white, star-shaped flower, common around old leadmines, as it is tolerant of the poisonous metal.

The toll road up to Scar House Reservoir has some lovely groups of common spotted orchid, as well as harebell, melancholy thistle and St John's wort.

Damp riverbank *(walks 3, 4, 7, 8, 12, 14, 16 and 19)* Alder and willow trees which like a wet situation line the riverbank. The alder was one of the first to colonise the land after the ice age and is still very common in Nidderdale; its wood has been used for clog-making and broom handles. The roots of both alder and willow help to bind the soil of the banks together and avoid erosion.

In spring, butterbur and sweet cicely are two easily-recognised riverside plants. Fat pink spikes of butterbur appear in March and April, the huge leaves developing later. The white flowers of sweet cicely appear in May, and can be identified by a strong smell of aniseed. The leaves can be added when cooking rhubarb so that less sugar is needed. By summer, rosebay willowherb, Himalayan balsam and pink purslane bring shades of pink to the riverside. These last three are introduced species, having escaped into the wild from gardens. Himalayan balsam is also known as policeman's helmet because of the flower shape, but it has also been named 'jumping jack' as the ripe seed pods snap open as you disturb

Because the seed pods of Himalayan balsam (lower left of drawing) spring open when touched to distribute their seeds, one name for the plant is 'jumping jack'.

25

The yellow and red-spotted flowers of the blood drop emlets are easily recognised in streamside situations.

them, scattering the seeds about. Dame's violet is another riverbank flower, the tall stems with a head of white or violet flowers being easily seen from a distance.

Other streamside plants include New Zealand willowherb, a diminutive member of this family often found by moorland streams; marsh speedwell, a creeping plant with very pale blue, almost white flowers; common figwort, which grows to about two feet (60cm) with small reddish-brown flowers; monkey flower, with bright yellow flowers and its cousin blood drop emlets, yellow with red blotches; wood stitchwort, a tall stitchwort with delicate white flowers; and shining cranesbill, a small, shiny-leaved geranium. Two most elegant and attractive flowers which thrive by Blayshaw Gill are giant bellflower, with tall spikes of milky blue flowers and melancholy thistle, a non-prickly thistle with fine purple heads.

Magnesian limestone *(walks 1 and 3)*

Soils are deep and fertile along the limestone belt and make good agricultural land,

and hedgerow plants give a good indication of where there is limestone below.

Hawthorn is the most common away from the limestone, but as soon as you get onto it again there is a great variety of shrubs, including the spindle tree, buckthorn, maple, dogwood and hazel, as well as climbing plants such as white and black bryony. The spindle tree is rather an inconspicuous small tree or bush, though in the autumn its narrow, pointed leaves turn red and it displays pinkish, four-lobed seed capsules. The hard, dense wood was used to make spindles, used by 'spinsters' (mostly unmarried girls) who spun wool on them. Dogwood also has red leaves in the autumn, broader than those of the spindle tree, with clusters of black berries. The buckthorn is a thorny shrub that also has black berries.

In waste corners of fields or disused quarries, there is a rich flora that includes kidney vetch, hairy St John's wort, salad burnet and agrimony. Kidney vetch is of the pea family, with a dense yellow flowerhead. The star-shaped flowers of hairy St John's wort are pale yellow and the leaves downy. Salad burnet is edible and the broken leaf smells of cucumber. Agrimony forms slender yellow spikes, each flower having notched petals.

Deciduous woodland *(walks 1, 2 and 4)*

On the steep slopes of the Nidd Gorge *(walk 4)*, wet patches have marsh marigold, golden saxifrage, watercress and wood rush; while in grassy places with broken shade grow wood sanicle, wood speedwell, wood sorrel and enchanter's nightshade. By the river among the alders are marsh willowherb, water forget-me-not, yellow loosestrife and monkey flower.

Birkham Wood *(walk 1)* — though now divided by a new road — is a botanically valuable area of ancient woodland, with spring delights of wood anemone, dog's

Some of the fungi to be found in Nidderdale. Top left is the hairy or boot-lace fungus, found on a variety of timber. Next to it is the bay bolete; the greenish-yellow pores turn blue on touching. Top right is the birch bracket fungus or birch polypore; its firm flesh and velvety texture give it the name of 'razor strop'. Below left is fly agaric, lovely to look at but very poisonous. Next is false chanterelle, found on both moors and in conifer woods. Then, the white helvella, with its fluted stem and convoluted cap, and only found in the lower dale. Bottom right is the deceiver; it has many different forms and so is not easy to identify.

27

mercury, bluebell, sweet violet and wild arum, and in the autumn a wide variety of fungi including the poisonous fly agaric and death cap, several milk caps and many colourful species of Russula.

Hedgerows and roadsides *(many of the walks)* Along the roadside near How Stean grow moschatel, an unusual, greenish-yellow flower, also known as town hall clock; wild arum or cuckoo pint, which produces an attractive spike of bright red berries in the autumn; betony, the attractive reddish-purple flowers growing well on drier banks; and rue-leaved saxifrage on limestone walls, a small plant with tiny white petals and three-lobed leaves, often reddish in colour.

The vivid yellow flower of leopard's bane.

Other roadside plants higher up the dale include leopard's bane, a tall, bright yellow, daisy-like flower that can be seen on the lane between Ramsgill and Bouthwaite; wood cranesbill, a geranium with large pinkish-purple flowers, self heal, including white variety, primroses, bugle, lousewort, common spotted orchid, crosswort, and bistort.

Lower down the valley, common wayside flowers include: cow parsley, that lacy white member of the parsley family which grows in masses along the verges; garlic

Wood cranesbill, a lovely native geranium, has pinkish-purple flowers with white centres.

mustard, an upright plant with white flowers, the crushed leaves of which smell like garlic; mugwort, a large, dowdy-looking plant with grey-green leaves and a touch of yellow in its crowded flower-heads; white deadnettle and yellow archangel with nettle-like leaves; the smaller ground ivy, a creeping plant with purple flowers; germander speedwell, the brightest of the blue speedwells; and pink purslane, an introduced plant of five-petalled, pink flowers and shiny green leaves.

Among its wide variety of flowering plants, fungi, ferns and trees, Nidderdale holds a lot of surprises for the interested observer. Even the casual walker cannot fail to notice some of the more outstanding or unusual plants along the wayside, and finding out the names of some of them can give much personal satisfaction.

WALK 1: GOLDSBOROUGH AND PLUMPTON ROCKS

Start: Goldsborough. Grid Ref: 381 561
Distance: 9 miles (14½ km)
OS Maps: Pathfinder 663 or Landranger 104
Walking Time: 5 hours

This is a walk on easy tracks and footpaths through rich farmland with scattered woodland , a walk to stretch the legs in a leisurely, rural part of the lower Nidd. Goldsborough, Plumpton and Ribston have rich histories, and the attractive and scenic area of Plumpton Rocks has been a local beauty spot for over 200 years. There is a small charge for entry to Plumpton Rocks, only open to the public on Saturdays and Sundays from noon until 5.00pm, but also open during Easter week (they are the reserve of fishermen the rest of the time). There is roadside parking in Goldsborough village, which lies south of the A59, only 2½ miles (3km) from Knaresborough. The Bay Horse Inn serves good food and has a large car park to the rear.

The small, peaceful, residential village of Goldsborough, built on limestone, has an ancient church, an Elizabethan hall, a first school and the Bay Horse Inn. Some of the buildings are of faded red brick and others, including the church and hall, are of contrasting pale grey limestone. The village lies exactly on latitude 54° north, the fifty-fourth parallel.

The name of Goldsborough has been fancifully interpreted as 'place of the gods'. It is mentioned in *Domesday Book* of 1086 as Godenesburg, 'Godel's fortification'. From the mid-twelfth century it became the seat of the Goldsborough family, who took their name from the village. In 1587 the ancient hall was destroyed, after which the Huttons acquired the estate and Richard Hutton built the fine mansion that still exists today. In the 1920s the hall became the first Yorkshire home of the Princess Royal after her marriage to Lord Lascelles (later Earl Harewood), when Queen Mary was a regular visitor. Goldsborough Hall is now a nursing home.

Next to Goldsborough Hall stands St Marys Church, which still retains a good example of a Norman doorway on the south side, with a row of beaked heads on the

round arch. It is possible that the church was built on an older holy site, as in the churchyard is a huge shaped rock known as the Fount Stone, the base of a ninth-century stone cross where annual payments of rent were made. The tower dates from about 1430. Inside the church (key with local resident), a chest-tomb below a stone canopy has the figure of Sir Richard Goldsborough (died in 1308), a knight in full Crusader's chain armour, while opposite lies a similar effigy of his son, who died about 1332. The stone carvings are exceptionally fine and well-preserved. Tradition links them with the Knights Templars of Ribston. Beautiful marble figures of Faith and Hope on the monument to Robert Byerley are the work of Joseph Wilton, sculptor to George III. When the Princess Royal was in residence, the Sunday service was very well-attended with people from all around wanting to see the royals, who entered by the door with the Norman arch.

Starting from the memorial, walk down the road past Avenue House Farm — built of limestone with a pantile roof — and a duck pond on the left. The farm track, lined with poppies, prickly sow thistle and mayweed, is known as Mill Road as it leads

A female linnet with her young. The linnet is a little brown bird, the male having a red forehead and breast, and in summer a chestnut-brown back with grey head. Their name comes from 'lin', an old word for flax, the seeds of which were thought to be the bird's favourite food.

in half a mile or so (1km) to Goldsborough Mill. The fields on each side may be sown with wheat, barley, sugar beet, potatoes or rape seed. The mill (now a farm) once employed specially-imported 'Niedermendig' mill stones, made of a hard lava and known for their milling qualities even to the Romans. The River Nidd runs in a shallow gorge where the magnesian limestone is seen to lie on millstone grit and where, in summer, dame's violet and Himalayan balsam adorn the banks.

Walk up the lane to the road where a roadside footpath, via road crossings, leads to the far side of the roundabout and an embankment, decorated in summer with red poppies. Go through the wooden gate and alongside the hedge (above the caravans) to enter Birkham Wood, with a view of a bend of the River Nidd below. This ancient woodland contains a wealth of plant

species. Early in the year, wood anemone, sweet violet, dog's mercury, bluebell and wild garlic predominate, while later, herb bennet, wood avens and the occasional orchid may be seen. Guelder rose and white bryony produce bright red berries in the autumn, the season for fungi, of which there are a great variety, including the striking fly agaric, the fairytale toadstool — red with white spots.

Cross the new road, which in spite of strong opposition has cut a broad swath through the centre of this irreplaceable wood, and eventually turn right along a field edge of blackthorn, hawthorn, bramble and wild rose. This is a good habitat for the wall butterfly — now fairly common in lowland parts of the Nidd Valley — and you may see its deep orange colour as it settles on the bare footpath in front of you in the sunshine.

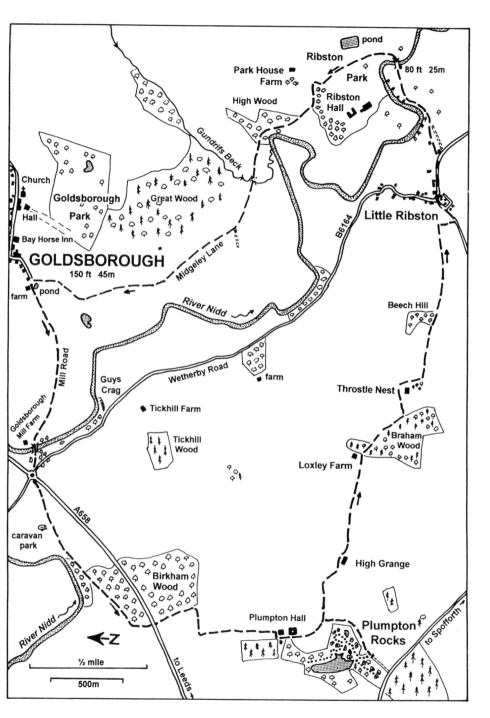

pond

Ribston

Park House ■ Farm

Park

80 ft   25m

High Wood

Ribston Hall

Church

Goldsborough Park

Great Wood

Little Ribston

B6164

Gundrifs Beck

Hall

Bay Horse Inn

GOLDSBOROUGH

150 ft   45m

farm   pond

Midgeley Lane

River Nidd

Beech Hill

Mill Road

Guys Crag

Wetherby Road

farm

Throstle Nest

Goldsborough Mill Farm

Tickhill Farm

Tickhill Wood

Braham Wood

Loxley Farm

A658

caravan park

Birkham Wood

High Grange

River Nidd

←-Z

Plumpton Hall

Plumpton Rocks

to Spofforth

½ mile

500m

to Leeds

Plumpton Hall, once part of Lord Harewood's estate, is now a large farmhouse with an impressive courtyard, the buildings around which have been converted to cottages.

The next field is called Great Harbour and the track leads to the large working farm of Plumpton Hall. A plaque low in a wall reads 'The Coach House 1770', and the fine courtyard is now converted to cottages. The farmhouse is particularly imposing, and it was formerly part of Lord Harewood's estate that once reached the ten miles (16km) from Harewood House, north of Leeds, all the way to Goldsborough and Flaxby.

At the junction of tracks, take the right fork for Plumpton Rocks. (The walk returns to this point before continuing further along the other fork.) Plumpton Park was laid out by Daniel Lascelles, who purchased the estate in 1753. Until then Plumpton Towers had been the family seat of the Plumptons for 560 years — since the time of William the Conqueror. Plumpton Towers was described by Leland in about the 1530s as 'a fair house of stone with two towers'. The building was pulled down in 1760 and never rebuilt, when Daniel

Lascelles went to live at his newly-acquired Goldsborough Hall.

Plumpton Rocks offer a fascinating and wonderful display of rock formations, naturally sculptured in millstone grit, with overhangs, deeply sunken paths, miniature gorges and a peaceful lake in an attractive wooded setting. On the lake you may see Canada geese, coot, tufted duck and mallard, while grey wagtails chase about the rocks. The trees include oak, beech, silver birch, scots pine, yew and rhododendron, and there is a variety of ferns on the woodland floor and in rock crevices. This peaceful wood is also a sanctuary for the shy roe deer and willow tit.

Return to the junction of paths and turn right to High Grange, a farm where asparagus and sweetcorn are specialities. Pass to the left of the farmhouse and on to Loxley Farm, going to the right of the house and through Braham Wood. Potatoes, broad beans and sugar beet are grown in this area. The wood is mainly of oak and ash, and the path is lined with elderberry. The concrete road leads round to Throstle Nest, a pig farm. Go beyond the house to the end of the road, turn right and then left along the hedge-side to Beech Hill. A damp field corner has been planted with willow, and mayweed and pineapple weed have covered bare ground. The two plants are similar, but the latter has no white petals and smells of pineapple.

Continue below a small wood on Beech Hill to cross two cornfields and a signed right turn to join the road and Little Ribston village. The village has lost its post office and there is neither shop nor pub. Turn right along the road (B6164) and left along South Park Lane. After the last cottage, a kissing gate leads the path forward to join the drive through Ribston Park to Ribston Hall. Cross the River Nidd on a balustraded stone bridge, from which there is a good view of the river, still not very wide. From here it embarks on a course of broad sweeping meanders before joining the River Ouse at Nun Monkton. The bridge is the lowest point on the walk (and of all the walks in this book) at eighty feet (25m) above sea level.

Ribston is famous for its connection with the Knights Templars. In 1217 land was given by Robert de Ros to this powerful and wealthy order of military monks who built a community house here, known as a preceptory. They wore white cloaks with a red cross on the front. Their aim was to guard the Holy Sepulchre in Jerusalem and to entertain pilgrims to the Holy Land. The order was suppressed in the early fourteenth century.

The distinguished Goodricke family came into possession of the manor of Ribston after the dissolution and held it for three centuries. The present Ribston Hall was rebuilt by Sir Henry Goodricke in 1674. A good view of the hall and chapel is seen from the public footpath. The extensive grounds contain many unusual trees, but perhaps the most famous is an apple tree called the Ribston pippin, seeds of which were brought from France around 1690. By the nineteenth century it was the most widely-grown of all the apple varieties. To the right a rectangular depression in the ground, thought to have been a jousting court, is now a newly-established lake that attracts tufted duck, shelduck, moorhen and coot, while oystercatchers and swallows are also drawn to it.

The waymarked path passes through a wooden gate and, just before Park House Farm, descends along a green, fenced track to High Wood and river level again. Here in June, blue and green damselflies dance among the vegetation. These attractive creatures look like small dragonflies but have a much weaker flight and, like dragonflies, catch insects on the wing with their bristly forelegs.

Carry straight on over a small stone bridge on a good track that passes through cultivated fields of wheat, barley and rape seed, turning right into the tarred Midgeley Lane. The hedgerows are the haunt of yellowhammers and linnets, two seed-eaters that stay with us all year. The yellowhammer rarely travels far from its territory, singing its jingling song from February through to August, and in winter you may see them feeding in the stubble and ploughed fields. The male is a vivid yellow, especially in the breeding season, the head being almost entirely lemon-yellow. The chestnut rump of both sexes is a useful distinguishing mark. The linnet is another attractive bird; the male has a red forehead and breast, with a grey head and chestnut back. It sings its twittering song from March to July, often delivered from the topmost twig of a bush.

The lane leads directly back to Goldsborough village.

WALK 2: HAY-A-PARK AND CONEYTHORPE FROM KNARESBOROUGH

Start: *High Street, Knaresborough. Grid Ref: 350 571*
Distance: *7½ miles (12km)*
OS Maps: *Pathfinder 663 or Landranger 99*
Walking Time: *4 hours*

This walk passes by Hay-a-Park gravel pits, known locally as the 'quarry ponds', a haven for waterfowl. The easy-to-follow tracks bring you through rich rolling farmland to Coneythorpe, where the Tiger Inn serves bar lunches (except Mondays). The return route, with broad views of Harrogate, gives a second chance for birdwatching on the ponds, before re-entering Knaresborough. Situated close to Harrogate, the town of Knaresborough is just six miles from the A1. York Place car park is free except on Wednesdays (market day in Knaresborough).

Knaresborough is one of Yorkshire's most beautiful old market towns. Situated on high ground overlooking the gorge of the River Nidd, it is the perfect setting for a Norman castle, historic church, and the ancient buildings and cottages that cling to the steep limestone crag.

The town is full of history. In 1170 it was in Knaresborough Castle that the four knights who murdered Thomas Becket, the Archbishop of Canterbury, took refuge. Their leader was Hugh de Morville, the then lord of Knaresborough. On several visits in the early 1200s, King John stayed here in the castle, and in 1210 he gave money to the poor of the town — the first recorded Maundy Thursday. Geoffrey Chaucer, whose son became constable of the castle, may have visited the town, while Richard II is the castle's most famous prisoner. The town also has its own saint, one Robert Flower, who gave up his worldly wealth for a pious life in a home in the rock, now St Robert's Cave.

To start the walk, go down High Street and turn right at the pedestrian crossing, along Raw Gap, to see the railway line emerge from a short tunnel. The line runs from Leeds to York, the old London North Eastern Railway. Cross Stockwell Road and continue on the left of the railway line above

garden allotments. After passing along the edge of a football field, turn right on Halfpenny Lane, then left and half-left between extensive glass-houses, along a footpath signed 'Sweet Bits'. The farm stands next to the former Hay-a-Park gravel pits — the quarry ponds. The extracted gravel was part of a former pre-glacial riverbed.

Before you get there, sounds of ducks and geese can be heard, for this is an important site for wildfowl. Walk down to the edge of the lake for some birdwatching. Both common and rare wetland birds may be seen: Canada goose, coot, tufted duck, mute swan, mallard and oystercatcher all breed here. You may see the handsome great-crested grebe perform its courtly display, a kind of neck dance. Large numbers of sand martins, house martins and swallows congregate here in the summer. You may also see common or Arctic terns. It is difficult to distinguish between these two when they are referred to as 'comic' terns (combining the words common and Arctic); they are most often seen in spring and autumn. In winter, large assemblies of pochard, goosander and black-headed gull may be present, and you never know what odd rarities might turn up just when you happen to be passing, so have a bird book handy.

It was the Normans who first built a castle at Knaresborough, and in the following centuries it served as a royal residence. During the Civil War the castle was captured by the Roundheads and later 'slighted', or partly demolished, on the orders of Oliver Cromwell. Today the picturesque ruins, and the magnificent view of Knaresborough from them, are a major tourist attraction.

35

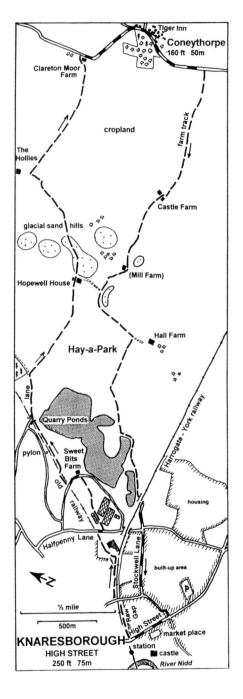

The route continues to the left of Sweet Bits Farm across fields to the right of the tall pylon, where a large field slopes down to the lake, another chance to see some of the water birds. The path then climbs to a stone bridge over the former railway line from Knaresborough to Boroughbridge. On the rougher ground in early summer you may see one or two delicate flying insects, the common blue and blue-tailed damselflies, some paired in a mating position.

From the bridge, continue along Hazelheads Lane, a hedge-lined track, turning off to the right through a wooden gate. In spring, wild daffodils adorn the fields here, which later have a colourful display of summer flowers — purple spikes of betony, the dandelion-like cats-ear and purple-headed knapweed. Linnets are attracted to the seeds of the last two and may be seen feeding on flower heads.

Straight on, one of the fields is often in white clover, and set with bee-hives to collect the honey. A shrub in the hedge is field maple, rare higher up the dale, and a field corner has been planted with young trees to make a small reserve. They include crab apple, oak, cherry and dog rose.

Pass the old brick building of Hopewell House Farm on the right. The last corn-crake in Nidderdale was heard in 1984. The path rises up and follows a sandy ridge of land, part of the lateral moraine of the Vale of York ice sheet. Over to the left, two rounded hills, called Near and Far Andrew Hill, are also of glacial sands on the same moraine. They provide well-drained soils for crops of linseed. In July the fresh green foliage of the flax acquires a beautiful pale blue haze, but by autumn turns dark brown. When the flax is in flower, the path is dotted with red poppies, tiny field pansies and the wiry stems of hedge mustard. The latter is not used in the kitchen, but in France it was renowned for giving a choirboy an

Hilary Roper.

The sparrowhawk may be seen on the hunt for small birds. The male measures only eleven inches (28cm), though the female is noticeably larger,. It has a grey back, a lightly-barred breast and bright yellow legs and feet. This fast-moving, low-flying hunter will dash along one side of a wall or hedge and flick over to the other side in a surprise attack.

37

angel's voice, and actors and singers there have taken potions of it to try to improve their voices.

A hedge-lined track leads through fields of cereals, and the path almost reaches the Hollies before turning sharply to the right through fields of wheat, barley and rape seed to Clareton Moor Farm. At field corners grow pineapple weed and wild radish and, just before the farm, white bryony swarms over the hedge. This climbing plant has ivy-shaped leaves, droopy clusters of green male flowers and short-stemmed, smaller female flowers that produce poisonous red poisonous berries in the autumn. It is more common in the south and west of England. Moorhens breed by a pond to the left, partridge may suddenly fly up, showing their distinctive orange tail, while a sparrowhawk might be seen preying on one of the smaller bird species such as the swallows that abound near the farm.

Pass to the left of Clareton Moor Farm and turn right along the road into Coneythorpe village, a quiet community with red-brick houses round a large green and water pump, overlooked by the Tiger Inn. An old directory of 1822 says that the name was formerly Kingsthorpe. Coneythorpe suggests that rabbits were bred here.

Carry on down the road, where the purple heads of tufted vetch mix with the yellows of meadow vetchling and agrimony. (It is preferable to walk along the road to the farm track, until the field path is improved.) A right turn through cereals, linseed and broad beans leads to Castle Farm. The hedge and verge provide a corridor for wildlife and summer flowers. The two tall willowherbs — rosebay and the more downy, greater willowherb — grow in clumps, along with dull-purple spikes of hedge woundwort, that foul-smelling hedgerow flower with soft furry leaves, once used for dressing wounds. Delicate lesser stitchwort, meadowsweet and wild roses add a sweeter scent. There are still a few wild patches by ponds, ditches and field corners where the natural environment prospers. The path passes over a ditch that is the haunt of the largest and most attractive of our voles, the water vole, now rarely seen higher up the Dales.

Turn right through the buildings at Castle Farm and forward along the field edge. The fine barn is constructed of magnesian limestone, while lesser buildings are of brick and rounded cobbles of gritstone. Further on, pink flowers of field bindweed grow in the path. Mill Farm now lies derelict, overgrown by nettles, and yellow stonecrop grows on the roof.

Over to the right is the cream-coloured building of Hopewell House, passed earlier in the walk. Continue along the tarred lane, where neatly-clipped hedges become grown over with goosegrass, that plant of the bedstraw family which children like to play with as it sticks so easily to clothing, a common name being cleavers. It is certainly edible to geese, and has medicinal uses, as it is related to coffee and quinine; roasted seeds have been used to make a coffee substitute.

Ahead is a view of the tall spire of Holy Trinity Church in Knaresborough. Just before Hall Farm, turn right over a wooden stile along the left side of a field hedge, then left along a tree-lined ditch. Cross this line of trees to continue following the ditch until you reach the Hay-a-Park gravel pits again, with a left turn alongside the water. On this side there is more cover for the birds, with willows along the shore and tall reed beds.

Pass under the railway arch, and keep straight on at Stockwell crossroads along Stockwell Lane to return to the centre of Knaresborough.

WALK 3: KNARESBOROUGH RIVER WALK

Start: _Market Place, Knaresborough. Grid Ref: 350 570_
Distance: _5 miles (8km)_
OS Maps: _Pathfinder 663 or Landranger 104_
Walking Time: _3 hours or more_

Here is a leisurely stroll along Knaresborough's scenic gorge, a most beautiful stretch of river, full of interest and reminders of past events, personalities and historic places associated with the town. Peaceful woodland and rocky crags are botanically rich and of geological importance. The walk is mostly on the level but there are one or two steep sections. There is a large car park by the river at High Bridge, and in the town the largest is off York Place, opposite the swimming pool (free except on Wednesdays).

Knaresborough is one of Yorkshire's most beautiful historic towns. Its splendid situation high above the Nidd — its name means 'fortress on the rock' — was no doubt appreciated early on by visiting Brigantes or Romans. The Angles certainly settled here and gave it the 'borough' part of its name. But it was not until the Normans built a castle and a church here, and laid out the plan of a market town, that the rich history of Knaresborough began to unroll. The history is enthusiastically described by Arnold Kellett in his book _Historic Knaresborough_.

Begin the walk in the attractive market place, where a market has been held every Wednesday since 1310. Above the general bustle, you may hear the town crier proclaiming the virtues of the town from the market cross. Until 1963 the square was completely cobbled. Look out for the Oldest Chemist's Shop in England, which has been in use since 1720, and on the other side, the town hall built in 1862.

From the corner of the market place, go down Kirkgate (opposite the information centre) which, as the name suggests, leads to the parish church. The tall church tower is topped by an unusual small spire. The peal of eight bells is rung on Tuesday evening and, in the past, helped to guide people coming through the Forest of Knaresborough on the eve of market day. Of particular interest inside are the font and its elaborately-carved cover, the fifteenth century nave and the Slingsby Chapel, which contains several tombs, including that of Sir Henry Slingsby who was beheaded by Cromwell for his loyalty to Charles I.

Return to descend the cobbled Waterbag Bank, so named because the town's water supply was once carried up here in leather bags on horseback. A plaque on a cottage on the left indicates the birthplace of Lord Inman of Knaresborough, who became chairman of the BBC and Lord Privy Seal. At the bottom of the hill is Manor Cottage, the only thatched cottage left in the town, while on the other side of Waterside is the Old Manor House, a Tudor building that belonged to the Roundheads and where Oliver Cromwell is said to have slept.

Continue along Waterside, past rowing boats and restaurants, to High Bridge. Cross the road and continue through the grounds of Conyngham Hall, an eighteenth-century building, once the home of Lord Mackintosh of Halifax, famous for his toffee. There are pleasant gardens with some lovely trees, and facilities for putting, bowls and tennis. Beyond the hall, aim for

Knaresborough's railway viaduct, 90 feet (30m) high and 338 feet (110m) long, as seen from from the bank of the River Nidd. It dates from 1851, and replaced the original viaduct of 1848, which collapsed into the river before it was finished. There was no loss of life, though fish were killed by the lime in the mortar.

the wooden bridge built on a natural rock-step in the river, cross and turn left to find a good riverside footpath in the downstream direction in woodland bordering Toffee Park. About 100 yards (90m) below the bridge, coarse millstone grit sandstone shows a steep easterly dip below the younger magnesian limestone (seen later). The path continues through the wood and along the riverbank back to High Bridge.

Cross the bridge and return to Waterside, which leads along the left bank of the river to Low Bridge. Pass first under the fine Victorian railway viaduct that carries the Harrogate to York line. The original

viaduct was built in 1848, but collapsed into the river when almost completed. This solid-looking replacement was finished in 1851. The cliffs on the left show splendidly the unconformity between the rather dull millstone grit below and the orange-coloured magnesian limestone above. Before the limestone was laid down, the whole of the coal measure strata had been deposited on top of the millstone grit and, in this area, eroded away again. The junction between the two rock types — the unconformity — represents a gap in time of about sixty million years.

Just beyond the steep cliffs, there is a

The view of the Nidd Gorge from Knaresborough Castle is rightly celebrated: the houses clinging to the hillside, pleasure boats on the river, the castellated railway viaduct, and the parish church in the distance.

weir across the river that provided water-power for Castle Mill, built in 1791, mainly used to make linen based on the local flax industry. The high-quality linen was supplied to all the royal household, and weaving continued until 1972. Beyond the car park is a view across the river of the Dropping Well. Lime-charged water drips down from the overhang and evaporates from objects hung there, eventually covering them with limestone (or tufa) in the same way that a stalactite is formed. Mother Shipton's Cave is nearby, close to the Long Walk. Mostly folk-tale, she is said to have been born in 1488, was deformed, and made many prophecies that came true. Prince Rupert apparently saw the Great Fire of London as a fulfilment of Mother Shipton's prophecy.

Low Bridge, formerly known as March

41

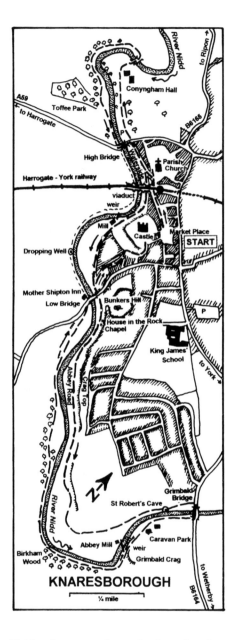

KNARESBOROUGH

¼ mile

Mother Shipton Inn on the far side of the
river and the Half Moon Inn on this side.
Cross the road, pass the Half Moon and
continue along Abbey Road. On the left is
Bunkers Hill, a large old quarry in magnesian limestone, the source of much of the
building stone for the town, and now a caravan park. Beyond this is the House in the
Rock, cut in the rockface between 1770 and
1786 by Thomas Hill and his son, and
named Fort Montague. It is open to the
public and an exit at the top can take you
onto Crag Lane. Next door is the wayside
shrine, the Chapel of our Lady of the Crag,
cut in the cliff by John the Mason in about
1408. The figure guarding the entrance is
likely to be a Knight Templar. Wordsworth
visited the chapel in 1802, and wrote the
following lines:

> *I once beheld a Templar Knight . . .*
> *Employed in setting his sword free*
> *From its dull sheath — stern sentinel*
> *Intent to guard St Robert's cell . . .*

Near the chapel, the cliff has rows of
post holes which, until about 1840, held the
roofs of weavers' houses.

The cliffs further along show millstone
grit near the base. The reappearance of
gritstone here and again on Grimbald Crag
shows that the magnesian limestone must
have buried former hills and valleys in the
millstone grit landscape. Further on, a
plaque on a wall refers to the place where
Trinitarian friars built a small priory in
1252 in memory of St Robert.

St Robert's Cave is on the right beyond
Abbey Mill. About the year 1160, Robert
Flower was born in York of upper-class
parentage and, after living with the Cist-
ercians for a time, eventually came to
Knaresborough to settle as a hermit in the
cave here on the bank of the Nidd. After
many trials, this pious man gained much
respect in the neighbourhood with a reputation for helping the poor and making
miraculous cures. Many came to him for

Bridge, from a word meaning boundary, has
an old ford; alongside it, each Boxing Day,
is now the scene of a tug-of-war between
teams from the seventeenth-century

spiritual guidance; his most distinguished visitor being King John who visited the cave in the February of 1216, a year after signing the *Magna Carta*. After Robert's death, many pilgrims came to visit his tomb, which was said to have flowed with healing oil. In 1745, the cave received further distinction when it was the scene of the murder of Daniel Clark, a crime for which the able schoolteacher Eugene Aram was hanged at York four years later.

Carry on to Grimbald Bridge, crossing it to return along the far bank of the river. Beyond the caravans and Plompton Mill Farm, climb up the side of Grimbald Crag. The unconformity is seen again here at path level, with limestone resting on millstone grit which here forms a buried hill of gritstone. Masses of sweet violets, both purple and white varieties, grow here and lime-loving plants include the large purple flowers of common mallow, yellow spikes of agrimony and the sweet-smelling wild marjoram. In the crevices of the yellow limestone grows pellitory-of-the-wall, a plant with small green flowers.

On the other side of the weir is Priory Mill, complete with water wheel. Enter the woodland where Birkham Wood reaches down to the river. This is a peaceful area and seems far removed from the busy town. Keep an eye open for the blue flash of a kingfisher over the calm river, a bird most likely to be seen by the fishermen who take up their positions along the bank. Plump brown trout are the prize of skilled fly-fishing, while there is a good mixed fishery of chub, dace, roach and barbel for the coarse fisherman. Spring flowers include wild garlic, herb bennet, red campion, wood sanicle and wood stitchwort, while the taller common mallow and Himalayan balsam come into bloom at the height of summer.

Exit from the wood, and after passing a few houses and cottages, come out onto Low Bridge. Cross the bridge and enter Waterside, turning up the hill to the right at the first footway. This leads on to Castle Ings Road and Bebra Gardens on the left, named after Knaresborough's twin town in Germany and, at the top of the hill on the left, to the ruins of Knaresborough Castle.

The castle was once a royal residence, with twelve towers and a magnificent keep. Eminent people who have lived here include King John, the murderers of Thomas Becket (1170), Edward III, Queen Phillipa and her son John of Gaunt (from 1372). In 1399 Richard II was imprisoned here. After the Battle of Marston Moor in 1644, the castle was captured by the Roundheads and later demolished on the orders of Oliver Cromwell.

The view from the castle is outstanding: the houses appear through the trees, tier upon tier, the bare limestone shows through here and there, itself bedecked with ivy, moss and wild flowers, and the castellated railway viaduct, reflected in the waters of the Nidd, adds a centrepiece, while in the distance is the tower of the parish church, topped with its small spire. It is a memorable scene that has decorated many a calendar and picture postcard.

Walk through Castle Yard to return to the market place.

WALK 4: THE NIDD GORGE ABOVE KNARESBOROUGH

Start: *High Bridge, Knaresborough. Grid Ref: 345 571*
Distance: *7 miles (11km)*
OS Maps: *Pathfinder 663 or Landranger 104*
Walking Time: *4 hours*

This walk explores the scenic Nidd Gorge, rich in both botanical and geological interest; some three miles (5km) of it pass through riverside woodland where the quiet footpaths often cling to steep, thickly-wooded slopes. The gorge upstream from the town of Knaresborough is a conservation area where paths have been improved and signposted. It is a beautiful stretch of countryside and an important habitat for wildlife. There is a large car park by the river at High Bridge (for Conyngham Hall), where the A59 crosses the River Nidd. From Knaresborough market place, the bridge can be reached by walking down Kirkgate and Waterbag Bank.

At one time the River Nidd flowed north of its present position, then during the Ice Age the huge Vale of York glacier blocked its easterly course and a vast lake formed, temporarily dammed by the massive ice-sheet. Torrents of water spilled over from the lake and rapidly carved a deep, winding channel along the edge of the ice. The channel became so deep that the Nidd never went back to its old course, but now runs in this deep gorge 130 feet (40m) below the surrounding land.

In historical times the area became part of the Royal Forest of Knaresborough, created by the Normans and later, Bilton Park, a deer park for the gentry. To mark Queen Victoria's jubilee in 1887, a sulphur spring was tapped at Bilton Spa, in Spring Wood, and piped to a fountain at High Bridge opposite the Yorkshire Lass, then known as the George Hotel.

The Nidd Gorge Project was set up in 1982 to conserve and enhance the environment of the Nidd Gorge for the benefit of wildlife and visitors. It is run by Harrogate Borough Council with support from the Countryside Commission and local people. Footpaths have been waymarked, some new sections opened, eroded and impassable paths resurfaced, and two nature trails introduced.

Start the walk from High Bridge, passing the Yorkshire Lass pub to a path along the riverbank. The ancient bridge, according to Jervoise, the civil engineer, 'is certainly medieval'. It has four ribs under the original part, has twice been widened on the upstream side to the present 36 feet (11m) and still carries the heavy traffic of the A59.

Take the path up the hill (ignoring the one signed Conyngham Hall Trail). Pause at the top of the hill by a large oak tree. The little wood to the left is known as Toffee Park because it was given to the town by Lord Mackintosh. The two big trees with intertwined branches, a few paces to the left, are a beech and a Turkey oak. This native of southern Europe has hairy buds and bristly acorns, and the leaves are shiny but rough on the surface. It was probably planted by the Slingsbys of Bilton Hall two or three hundred years ago.

Carry straight on alongside a tall hedge. May and cherry blossom later give way to wild roses and bramble, with the yellow flowers of rough hawkbit, goat's beard and agrimony, while meadow brown butterflies jostle for position on the purple heads of knapweed. By July some of the goat's beard have produced their downy seed-heads, like a dandelion clock. Its alternative name is Jack-go-to-bed-at-noon, as the flower only opens in the morning.

On the right, through a line of oaks and limes, is a view of Bilton Hall. The Slingsby family occupied the hall from Henry VIII's time. But during the Civil Wars the Puritan Thomas Stockdale lived here, replacing the Royalist, Sir Henry Slingsby, who had been expelled from the House of Commons in 1642. Thomas Stockdale was also MP for Knaresborough but supported Cromwell. The hall was largely rebuilt in 1857.

Go forward along Bilton Lane which takes you, over a mile (1.8km) further on, to Old Bilton and Bilton Beck. Between the hall and Limekiln Plantation, the lane is on Permian marl, a red, clayey rock that produces poorly-drained, reddish soils. The old quarry in Limekiln Plantation was the source of magnesian limestone that was burned to make lime — used mainly to sweeten acid soils, but it was also important in the making of mortar for building purposes.

Pass between the scattered houses of Old Bilton and down the road to the bridge over Bilton Beck and the Gardeners Arms. Bilton is mentioned in *Domesday Book* in which it states, 'Gilbert Tyson has these lands, but they are all waste'.

Ignore the footpath to the right; instead, continue for another 200 yards (180m) and turn right onto the former railway line. In spring and summer the old track is full of birds, flowers and butterflies. Willow warblers, blue tits, great tits and the yellowhammer are all to be seen or heard, and there is a fine display of colour along this half mile (800m) of railway track. Rosebay willowherb is typical of railway embankments, and is the foodplant of the elephant hawk moth. The deep yellow birdsfoot trefoil comes earlier in the year, and is the foodplant of the common blue butterfly that

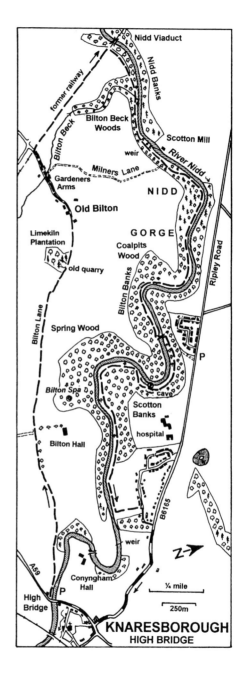

45

Hilary Roper.

Greater stitchwort is a straggly plant characteristic of oak woodland on acid soils. The white, starry flowers (½ inch, 1.2cm across) have five petals, each one divided for half their length.

you may see on the wing in June. Knapweed is common, as are clumps of dark green, dusty-looking mugwort. This last plant is slightly aromatic and was thought to have magical properties. It is said that if a coal was hidden beneath its roots, it would give protection from lightning, plague and carbuncles! Culpepper's *Herbal* says mugwort is excellent for female disorders, and that tea made from it will hasten delivery and help expel the afterbirth. Also common here are kidney vetch, which has a yellow pom-pom flower head; meadow vetchling, a more straggly member of the pea family, again with yellow flowers; and tufted vetch,

with striking dense blue flower-spikes. The lovely yellow flowers of perforate St John's-wort also decorate the track.

On approaching the river, walk on to the Nidd Viaduct for a view of the upper end of the gorge. Trains from Harrogate to Thirsk once crossed the Nidd here, 120 feet (36.5m) above the river. The view is impressive.

Continue high above the right bank of the river and descend to where Bilton Beck enters the Nidd at a wooden footbridge. Bilton Beck Woods is now managed by the Woodland Trust as a nature reserve. It is mainly broad-leaved, the oak being dominant, both sessile and pedunculate species. Acorns from pedunculate oaks have stalks and those from sessile oaks don't. There are also hybrids of the two. The oak attracts more insect life than any other tree and, therefore, altogether more wildlife. In spring, wood anemones, bluebells, greater stitchwort and wood sorrel give brightness and colour to the woods. They are characteristic of oak woodland on acid soils.

You may have heard the descending notes of the willow warbler along the old railway, but here you are likely to hear the less common chiffchaff. By sight, the two are very difficult to distinguish from each other, but the song is quite different. The up and down *chiff-chaff chiff-chaff chiff-chaff* call is easy to recognise. This hardy warbler arrives from southern Europe or Africa by the end of March, two weeks before the willow warbler, and does not leave till October.

The weir was built to give water power to Scotton Mill. An occasional grey wagtail or dipper may be seen near or below the weir where the river is faster-flowing. The path climbs over a river bluff, where there is an exposure of thinly-bedded Carboniferous sandstone and a small gully. The junction of paths is where Milners Lane comes down from the right. Keeping to the riverside, descend to a more open stretch, where boardwalks cross marshy ground; wild cherry, oak, alder, silver birch and willow are all young trees, and gorse and broom complete the shrubby landscape. The next bit of mature woodland is Coalpits Wood. There are still reminders of the coal workings in occasional craters in the wood, where shafts were sunk. The path climbs again above the river bluff of Bilton Banks, then further on there is a more open, grassy area with gorse, hawthorn and brambles, before more riverside woods with a 'coppiced' look and lots of bluebells in the spring. Hazel, sycamore, oak, willow and rowan are all present. When coppicing was carried on, it entailed cutting the trees down to just above ground level, and then letting them grow new shoots; after twenty-five years they would be cut again, providing poles for fencing and many other uses.

A boggy area and boardwalk just before the wooden footbridge over the river has meadowsweet and more Himalayan balsam, with alders growing on a small island. The cut timber of the alder tree is a deep blood-orange colour, which gave rise to the wide belief that the tree was evil and to be feared. The seasoned timber is yellow and used for clog-making, while the leaves and bark yield a dye.

Cross the fine wooden footbridge, from which there are good views up and down the river, and leave the Forest of Knaresborough. The Nidd formed the northern boundary of the royal Forest all the way from the Nidd Gorge to the other side of Little Ribston.

Turn right along the other bank of the river to climb a stepped path over the cliffs of Scotton Banks, where Jack Carter's Cave is hidden. For 90 yards (80m) join a wide forest road, before descending again to the river. On the forest road there are the tall pink blooms of common spotted orchid and hairy St John's-wort. The latter differs from perforate St John's-wort by its larger leaves, paler yellow colour, and black spots along the sepals and bracts; these small 'leaves' among the flowers have black glands on stalks along their margins which are well seen with a lens.

On the river, goosander and dipper or heron may be seen. But keep a look-out for the sparrowhawk on the hunt for small birds. It is a little larger than a kestrel, and flies fast and low through the trees. It has a grey back, a lightly-barred breast and bright yellow legs and feet; and it nests in this part of the wood.

Eventually you are forced to leave the riverbank where the path climbs to the road. Three right turns along the road bring you back to High Bridge, a distance of 1,000 yards (900m) on roadside footpaths.

WALK 5: HARLOW CARR AND BEAVER DYKE RESERVOIRS

Start: *Harlow Moor Road, Harrogate. Grid Ref: 288 547*
Distance: *11½ miles (18½km)*
OS Maps: *Pathfinder 663 or Landranger 104*
Walking Time: *5½ hours*

Here is a full day's outing that explores the valley of Oak Beck and Beaver Dyke reservoirs, an area known as Havarah Park, with a visit to John O' Gaunt's Castle. It is mostly easy walking on good tracks, and there is an opportunity for birdwatching. Start from the roadside car park in Harlow Moor Road (opposite the water works) on the west side of Harrogate. To reach there by car from the entrance to Valley Gardens, go along Cornwall Road or Valley Drive. If you prefer to start from the town centre and walk through the gardens, this adds 1½ miles (2½km) to the total distance.

Harrogate has a relatively short history. There was not much there in the late sixteenth century when William Slingsby wandered with his dog over the area now known as the Stray, and discovered the medicinal waters of Tewit Well. But, by the late eighteenth century, an elegant town and fashionable spa had grown up. In modern times Harrogate has become a residential town for Leeds and Bradford, but retains an important tourist attraction as 'the floral resort' and as a conference centre.

Bogs Field, now known as Valley Gardens, is the site of most of the sulphur and iron water springs, where thirty-six springs rise within a small area, each said to have different chemical properties. The springs emerge along the main fault that runs west to Harlow Carr.

Begin by walking up Harlow Moor Road from the car park, to where a path turns right through the trees to Crag Lane and Harlow Carr Gardens. Cross a clearing in the woods, then admire the views of the Oak Beck valley on the right.

Join Crag Lane, where straight ahead are the justly famous, landscaped botanical gardens of Harlow Carr, the headquarters of the Northern Horticultural Society. Begun in 1948, there are now sixty-eight acres

(28ha) of beautiful gardens, where practical aspects of horticulture are demonstrated and where threatened garden flowers and vegetables are conserved. The gardens are open all year, and a whole day should be set aside for a visit. The restaurant and plant centre are open to casual visitors (no charge).

Turn right for 150 yards (135m), then left. Just past the Harrogate Arms Hotel, the path continues on the side of a stream where you can detect the smell of sulphur. Rocks in the stream show vertical bedding, an indication of the nearness to the main fault from which the sulphur springs rise.

The gravel path leads through woodland, and after joining the Ringway footpath — keep straight on here — overlooks the deep valley of Oak Beck. Towards the end of the Ice Age, this valley carried overspill waters from Lake Washburn, making it much bigger than the present small stream could carve out. The beech woods in summer are the home of chiffchaff and willow warbler, two very similar warblers that can be distinguished by their song. The piping, descending notes of the willow warbler may be familiar, and the *tip-tap-tip-tap-tip* of the chiffchaff is a welcome sound from the less common of the two.

Further on, the woods are mainly of birch, and many trees display the bracket fungus of birch polypore or razor strop. The leathery, pale-brown growth juts out from the trunk, mainly on dying trees, and measures some six inches (15cm) across. Emerge onto the road at Pot Bank. Walk down over the bridge and up the other side, to turn left on a track through the yard of Pot Bridge Farm, and on, via other farms, to Oatlands. After the woodland of Oak Beck, here the surroundings change to open country where, for the next 2½ miles (4km), meadows alternate with grazing land and views across the valley, known as Havarah Park. The name is an old one and has a delightful story behind it. When John of Gaunt was lord of the Forest of Knaresborough, a cripple named Havarah asked him for a plot of land from which he could make a living. The request was granted in the following terms:

'I, John O' Gaunt,
Do give and do grant
to thee Havarah,
As much of my ground
As thou canst hop round
On a long summer day.'

The canny cripple chose the longest day, began hopping at sunrise and continued till evening. Just as the sun was setting, he completed the circuit by throwing his crutch across the gap to the point where he started, and so earned the land which still bears his name.

At Oatlands Farm turn right, through a metal gate, pass a wood on the left and follow it round through two wooden gates, in the up-valley direction again. The path runs alongside a good stone wall, then passes between two large working farms, Whin Hill and Prospect House. The next farmyard is that of Central House Farm. The grazing land is rougher and there are scattered clumps of gorse.

Swallows and pied wagtails frequent the

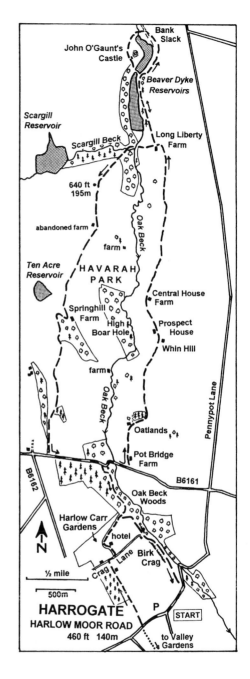

farms of Havarah Park, where they find a plentiful supply of insects in and around the farmyards; but you may also see goldfinches, which use tree cover and prefer rough ground or gardens where plants are allowed to seed. You may hear the call of the curlew as it patrols the open hillside, and you may also hear the nearby scolding *tic-tic* of the whinchat, or its short metallic song, delivered from a perch on a gorse bush or wire.

A short section of green lane leads to a road at Long Liberty Farm. Turn left, then right, for the first view of the first reservoir. This is the lower of the two Beaver Dyke reservoirs. Stocked with rainbow trout, it is popular with anglers for fly-fishing. Continue, with a larch wood on the left, down to a wooden gate near the lake. Through the trees you should see a few

birds on the water: great crested grebe, with long, slender neck, and handsome crest and head; tufted duck, a neat little duck with a white patch on its side and a wisp of a crest; and coot, black except for a white forehead. They all breed here, and it is worth looking out for the little grebe, too.

The upper reservoir soon comes into view, and the path climbs to an attractive viewpoint where a seat commemorates the golden jubilee (in 1985) of the Ramblers Association. You may have added grey heron, common sandpiper and grey wagtail to your list of water birds. Pass below a ruined farmhouse, following the path until opposite the end of the reservoir, at which point turn down to the left to two iron kissing gates. At the turning-down point, it is possible to make out the beginning of an earthwork called Bank Slack, a ridge of ground

The upper reservoir at Beaver Dyke, with the Ramblers' Association memorial seat in the foreground.

50

The great crested grebe is an expert diver, and is rarely seen out of the water. A large, slender-necked bird, in the breeding season it has a black crest and chestnut frills on each side of its head. Its nest is a floating platform built of weeds and attached to the reeds by the edge of a lake.

with a hollow alongside it that carries straight on (with path), a defensive line which may have been part of the enclosure of Havarah Park.

Curve round, following the field boundary, up to a ruined wall, which is all that remains of a farmhouse with some large fireplace stones, though nearby farm buildings still stand around a neat yard. On the mound to the left is John O' Gaunt's Castle, with a fine moat still in evidence and a solitary wall corner standing twelve feet (3.6m) high. The so-called castle is considered to have been a hunting lodge of John of Gaunt, Duke of Lancaster, who was lord

of the honour of Knaresborough for twenty-eight years to 1399; Thomas Chaucer, son of the poet, was his steward. Edward II stayed here for a few days in September 1323.

Looking out for the kestrel that nests nearby, descend to the dam, crossing over it, and retrace your steps to Long Liberty Farm. Turn right through a gate to descend and cross the beck below the dam. Follow the waterworks road for 200 yards (180m) alongside Scargill Beck, which runs down from Scargill Reservoir, the site of Pippin Castle (thought to have been a chapel of John O' Gaunt's Castle) and of an old Viking settlement — both now flooded. By a cattle grid, climb the south side of the valley to a ladder stile. The route continues diagonally up the field near a line of electricity poles.

If you keep a look-out ahead and to the left, you may see some orange-brown fur and two long, black-tipped ears that belong to a hare. This animal has excellent eyesight and hearing that give it warning of danger in its open habitat. It often sits up to survey its surroundings and will lope along unhurriedly, but in response to danger can run as fast as thirty-five miles (56km) an hour. Hares inhabit the next two fields on the left, where there are plenty of rushes and rough ground for cover.

Following the yellow arrows, pass an abandoned farm on the right. From the track are views over Havarah Park, a royal hunting park, owned for a long time by the Ingilby family of Ripley. It was no doubt well-stocked with deer, but the names of High Boar Hole and Low Boar Hole suggest that wild boar were a speciality. Perhaps it was here that Thomas Ingilby saved King Edward III from being savaged by a wild boar, a timely action that earned him a knighthood. A painting to commemorate the incident hangs in Ripley Castle. The rough grazing land is still home to lapwing, meadow pipit, skylark and kestrel.

Just before the gate and Springhill Farm, a rock by the track has a good example of the old style of benchmark with broad arrow and brass pin above it. The benchmarks and height are given on the old six inch (1:10,000) maps. To the right are the green slopes of the dam of Ten Acre Reservoir. The path curves round across the beck and up the other side. The woodland along the bottom — of oak, alder and birch — is the haunt of the green woodpecker, and you may hear its loud laughing call or 'yaffle'. The adult bird's dull-green back, red crown and black face are very distinctive while, in flight, the yellowish rump is a striking feature. It is a good tree-climber and wood-borer, with a strong bill and long, sticky tongue, climbing spirally up the trunk in jerky hops, though it often feeds on the ground seeking for ants.

On the far side of the wood, between the wood and the track, is an interesting bit of marshy ground where the pink flowers of ragged robin, dense spikes of common spotted orchid, in various shades of pink, and the golden-yellow blooms of bog asphodel all grow. All three flowers are to be found on wet ground and are in flower in early July. Bog asphodel is a member of the lily family, and grows on moors and mountains as far as the north of Scotland.

A rocky outcrop, on the left, has birch trees rooted in solid rock that shows some good cross-bedding, an indication that the sandy sediment was deposited by a strong current. The good track passes pine woods to the left, comes alongside a well-built estate wall and meets the main road, the B6161 from Pool to Ripon.

Turn left along the road for 700 yards (650m) down the hill to Pot Bank, where a right turn brings you along a path used earlier in the day through Oak Beck Woods. Join the Ringway footpath and follow it at a left turn, down over the wooden footbridge and up on a high-level path through the woods.

At the rocky outcrop of Birk Crag, the sandstones are seen to dip very sharply towards the valley (to the north-west), and are part of the steep northern limb of the Harrogate Anticline. In his *History of Harrogate*, William Grainge declares 'this is the grandest piece of scenery in the neighbourhood of Harrogate', and a little further along is a good viewpoint over the narrow valley of Oak Beck. After this the path descends, and eventually comes out on a bend in the road that leads up to Harlow Moor Road and the car park.

WALK 6: CAYTON GILL AND RIPLEY PARK

Start: *Ripley. Grid Ref: 284 605*
Distance: *6 miles (9½km)*
OS Maps: *Pathfinder 653 or Landranger 99*
Walking Time: *3 hours*

The attractive and fascinating 'continental' village of Ripley makes a good starting point. The church, castle and gardens are all well worth a visit. Making pleasant and easy walking, the route explores the picturesque valley of Cayton Gill, a glacial overflow channel with botanical interest. The route crosses to the valley of Ripley Beck, finally rounding the estate of Ripley Park, where a herd of fallow deer roams. Ripley lies just off the A61 (Harrogate/Ripon road). There is a large car park close to the village.

Ripley village was rebuilt in the mid 1820s by Sir William Ingilby, who planned it in the style of a French village he knew in Alsace Lorraine. The neat cottages look on to a tree-lined street and an open square with market cross and fountain. Sir William was also responsible for landscaping the area with the creation of two lakes, completed in 1844. The pretentious Hôtel-De-Ville, the village hall, was finished soon after his death in 1854.

The Ingilby family have lived in Ripley continuously since Thomas de Ingilby first arrived and married the heiress Edeline Thweng in about 1320. In 1355, when King Edward III was hunting in Knaresborough Forest, he was saved from the attack of a wild boar by the same Thomas, who received a knighthood for his chivalry. The boar's head became part of the family crest, and a stone sculpture of the beast stands in the centre of the village, opposite the new hotel of the same name.

Ripley Castle is really a manorial hall, complete with fortified gatehouse — built in 1415 as a defence against Scottish raids — and tower, erected in 1555, still with its rare oak 'waggon-roof' ceiling, spiral staircase and priest hole. In 1644, Royalist Sir William Ingilby and his sister, 'Trooper Jane' — dressed as a soldier with

a full suit of armour — raised a troop of horsemen from Ripley and joined the king's army. On the 2nd July they were routed at Marston Moor and Oliver Cromwell pursued the fleeing army to Ripley Castle, where he spent an unwelcome night. It is likely that the secret priest-hole was used to hide Sir William while Jane gave Oliver an uneasy night on the ground floor with a brace of pistols at the ready. Most of the mansion was sensitively rebuilt in the 1780s, and the priest hole remained a secret until 1963. The house, with many interesting treasures, and the lovely gardens and grounds are all open to the public.

The church of All Saints dates from about 1400 and contains several Ingilby tombs. It replaced an older one that was built too near the river and fell in a landslide in 1395. On the night Cromwell was here, he made use of the church to stable his horses, and on the outer east wall are bullet holes made by his troopers where they shot prisoners. In the churchyard is a pedestal of two stone blocks, thought to be the base of a thirteenth-century 'weeping cross', with niches to receive the knees of penitents.

From the Boars Head, walk up the street past the Hôtel-de-Ville and along an abandoned stretch of road to cross the Pateley

53

The Church of All Saints in Ripley was rebuilt around 1400 after the original building was damaged by a landslide. Its interior boasts examples of stained glass from some of the best designers of the Victorian era.

Bridge road (B6165) and on to Birthwaite Lane, opposite. After Birthwaite House, the lane becomes a farm track; fork right at the dividing of the ways to follow the Nidderdale Way and the blue arrows of a bridleway. The narrow lane passes between fields of cereals. In spring, white patches in the hedgerow belong to garlic mustard, white deadnettle and cow parsley. By late summer there are the purples of rosebay willowherb, knapweed and foxgloves, and the pink of persicaria occupy the ditch. The last flower, also known as redshank because of its red stems, is a garden weed related to bistort and the dock family.

The path draws close to a wood on the right, named Sir Henry Wood — presumably named after Sir Henry Ingilby —

54

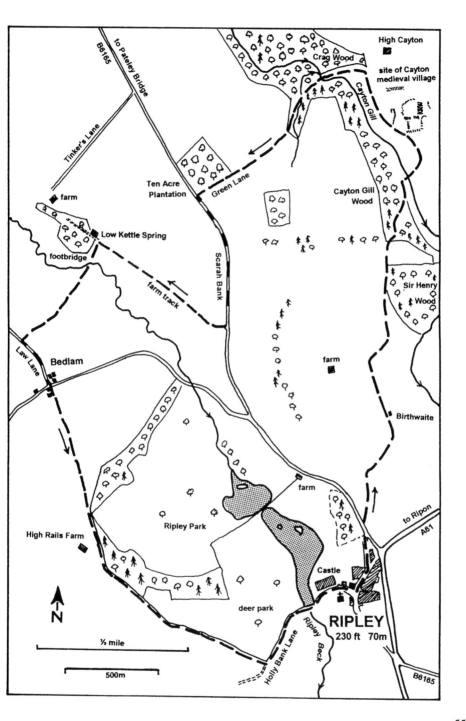

B6165

to Pateley Bridge

Tinker's Lane

farm

Ten Acre Plantation

Green Lane

Low Kettle Spring

footbridge

farm track

Scarah Bank

Law Lane

Bedlam

High Cayton

Crag Wood

site of Cayton medieval village

Cayton Gill

Cayton Gill Wood

Sir Henry Wood

farm

Birthwaite

High Rails Farm

Ripley Park

farm

to Ripon
A61

Castle

deer park

RIPLEY
230 ft 70m

Holly Bank Lane

Ripley Beck

B6165

N

½ mile

500m

55

Rapeseed in full bloom near High Cayton.

where pines are bordered by sycamores and bluebells. Fork right again for a lovely view down into the valley of Cayton Gill. There is a fine display of foxgloves on the wild slopes facing the gill. The clusters of glove-finger-shaped flowers — appropriately called 'finger hat' in German — hang on one side of the stem, forming a mass of pink. The drug digitalis is made from the leaves and is used to treat heart failure.

Descend through Cayton Gill Wood into the gill itself, crossing the little beck by a neat stone-arched bridge and bearing left along the top of a ridge up the right side of the valley. The floor of Cayton Gill is wide, flat and poorly drained, and the steep, wooded sides give it a secluded and pictur-esque appearance. During the Ice Age, this broad, winding channel was excavated by torrents of water overflowing from a lake

to the north that was ponded up against the York ice sheet. Ripley village actually stands on the delta, formed at the lower end of the channel. In summer, splashes of yellow among the rushes are the attractive, large 'daisy' heads of marsh ragwort. To the right is the site of the medieval village of Cay-ton, mentioned in the *Domesday* survey.

At the head of the gill, turn left along the edge of Crag Wood, where bluebells flourish in the spring.

You may notice two or three kinds of bumble-bee among the thistles along here, including the buff-tailed variety, with yel-low tail and two yellowish bands round the body. There is also a white-tailed species and one with an orange tail. Bumble-bees are more furry and live in smaller colonies than honey bees. Because they don't store honey, they die off as winter approaches,

56

and the young fertile queens hibernate to make a new colony in the spring. Along here I found a large fairy ring of robust toadstools, which must have taken several years to reach a diameter of some twelve feet (3.6m) across.

At the end of the pasture, go through the wicket gate and turn left to join a farm track. Pass the end of Cayton Gill Wood on the left, and further along Green Lane is Ten Acre Plantation. At the road, turn left for 330 yards (300m) down Scarah Bank, then right along a farm track to Low Kettle Spring. From here is a view of the vale of Thornton Beck, fed by streams from Brimham Moor.

Just before the farm buildings, turn left through a gate and go straight down the field to a hidden footbridge that straddles Thornton Beck. The path continues up along the field edge and a line of oak and ash trees, and up to Law Lane that leads left to Bedlam and Scarah Bank cottages. Go to the left of the house and the automatic gates opposite, along the margin of three or four fields where cattle may be grazing, eventually following the boundary wall of Ripley Park, with High Rails Farm

on the right. The wall here also marks the border of the Forest of Knaresborough, Ripley Park being outside it.

By July, you may see the slender, yellow spikes of agrimony growing below the wall. A member of the rose family, each flower stays open for three days. An old name for it is Aaron's rod and the leaves have been used for herb teas. The plant likes lime and may receive some from the mortar in the stone wall. Curve round into Holly Bank Lane, where if you peep over the wall you may get a view of some fallow deer, for there is a herd of about eighty in Ripley Park. Of medium size, in summer they have a reddish-brown coat with spots and a white rump, edged with black. Towards the end of October the rut will be in full swing, when the larger bucks gather a harem of does, and rival bucks fight fiercely, charging each other with loud clashes of antlers. Holly Bank Lane lies along the course of the Roman road from Ilkley to Aldborough (through Ripley), which here became part of the old road from Lancaster to York.

The castle comes into view with the lakes below, and soon you return to the cobbled square.

WALK 7: PACKHORSE BRIDGE AND BURNT YATES FROM HAMPSTHWAITE

Start: *Hampsthwaite. Grid Ref: 260 588*
Distance: *6 miles (9½km)*
OS Maps: *Pathfinder 663 and 653 or Landranger 104 and 99*
Walking Time: *3 hours*

Starting from the large and attractive village of Hampsthwaite, the walk follows the River Nidd upstream for a short way, to cross the beautiful packhorse bridge that spans the river above Birstwith. There follows a steady climb up the sunny side of the valley to the ridge-top village of Burnt Yates, after which a descent brings the walker through Clint village — with its ancient cross — and down to Hampsthwaite Bridge. Hampsthwaite is not far from Harrogate and may be reached from the A59 (Harrogate/Skipton road). There is limited parking near the green or along the road between the green and the river.

Hampsthwaite, on the south side of the Nidd, centres on a triangular green with pub, post office, shop, garage and school. In Roman times, the road from Ilkley to Aldborough came through here, crossing the Nidd by a ford above the present bridge. About 1300 the village was granted a market charter, but the weekly market was not kept up. Being within the Royal Forest of Knaresborough, residents had to observe many rules.

By the eighteenth century a group of smiths at the top end of Hampsthwaite were already specialised in the manufacture of spurs. In making the spur, the 'rowel' or spiked wheel was of a particular local pattern, for which the spurs were noted. All being sold in Ripon, they became known as 'Ripon spurs', and one of them appears on the Ripon coat of arms. Other smiths made metal dishes and sieves.

Generations of Thackerays lived in the village, ancestors of William Makepeace Thackeray, author of *Vanity Fair*. One, Thomas Thackeray, became headmaster of Harrow School in 1746. Peter Barker was a notable inhabitant and a remarkable character who died in 1873 aged sixty-four. He became blind when a young boy, but nevertheless soon learned to play the fiddle,

playing at dances and fairs. He turned his skills to carpentry, made some fine pieces of furniture and also kept the church clock in working order. The composer Amy Woodforde-Finden lived some of her life in Hampsthwaite, and died here in 1919 to be buried in the churchyard. A fine, white marble monument in the church, carved by George Wade of London, is decorated with eastern scenes and topped by a beautiful effigy of the lady. She is remembered as composer of the Indian love lyrics such as *Far across the Desert Sands* and *Pale Hands I Loved Beside the Shalimar*.

From the green, walk down Church Lane past the school to the church. The route goes through the churchyard, so pause to look inside the building that was restored in 1901-02. The tower has survived from the late fifteenth century, and the church is dedicated to St Thomas Becket. The original building was founded about 1175 by William de Stuteville, brother-in-law to Hugh de Morville, who was involved in the murder of Becket in July 1170. It is possible that Stuteville wanted to clear his name from the terrible deed and so dedicated the church to Becket — canonised in 1173. Mounted on one wall is part of a fourteenth-century brass, the pulpit is

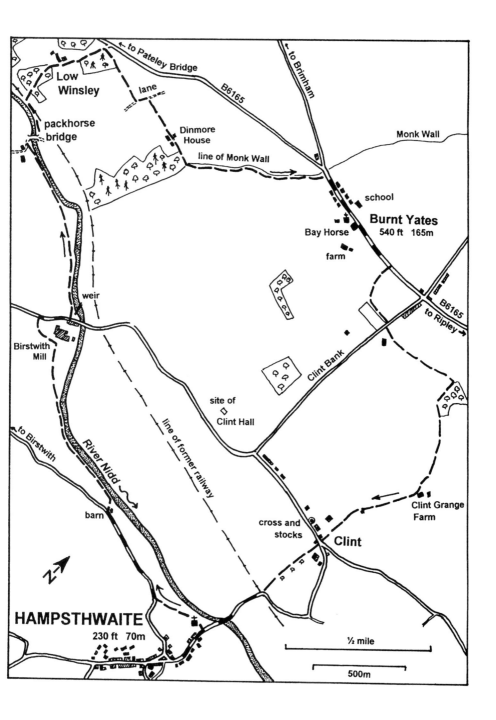

Jacobean, and oak panels have dates of 1671 and 1695 inscribed on them.

Continue the walk through the large churchyard and on to a paved churchgoer's path where pink purslane grows. After 600 yards (550m) along the road, turn off to the right on the far side of an L-shaped roadside barn and join the riverbank. The river water is most often stained brown from the peaty moors. The colouring persists even though the river is interrupted by three large reservoirs. However, it doesn't appear to affect the wildlife and you may see a dipper or moorhen along this stretch, a sure sign of the healthy state of the river. Fallen logs near the path have a velvety-brown, rubbery fungus growing on them known as Jew's ear or Judas' ear. The name refers to the story that Judas hanged himself on an elder, the ear being his returned spirit. In this case the dead timber may be elm.

Follow the re-routed path round Birstwith Mill, where Lucas Ingredients make rusk from wheat flour, and continue across the road along the mill race. On the slopes to the left is the village of Birstwith, dominated by the tall church spire. There are some fine oaks by the path and, on a mature cherry, grows a soft, spongy, yellow bracket fungus, known as sulphur polypore.

Arrive at the graceful arch of the beautifully-built packhorse bridge that crosses the Nidd in a single seventy foot (21m) span. There was a timber bridge here in the sixteenth century. The present one was

Cottages in Hampsthwaite. The smiths of the village were renowned for making spurs as well as metal dishes and sieves.

There has been a church in Hampsthwaite since the end of the twelfth century, and the tower dates from the fifteenth. The church itself was restored in 1901–02 by Hodgson Fowler.

built in 1822 and became known as New Bridge. It is still only a footbridge, being just 6 feet (1.8m) wide, has an attractive cobbled surface and leads to Burnt Yates via Tinkers Lane. Growing in the crevices of the bridge is a white variety of the normally pink herb robert. If you sit quietly you may catch a glimpse of a stoat that lives nearby. This slim, pale brown carnivore is creamy-white underneath with a black tip to its tail, and is a fierce predator. Make a squeak like a frightened rabbit and it will take an added interest in you.

Cross the bridge and continue up the far side of the river for two fields, then cross the line of the old railway (from Knaresborough to Pateley Bridge) where, by the middle of summer, there is a mass of rosebay willowherb, typical of railway embankments, together with the purple tops of knapweed, striking blue flowers of tufted vetch and the rather insignificant enchanter's nightshade, a relative of willowherb.

Cross into a mixed wood of young trees, where bluebells, wild garlic and forget-me-nots flourish. Pass the house and cottages of Low Winsley and up a tarred lane to the road. Here, turn right just before the road along the top edge of a pine wood. Keep the wall on the left, and turn left for 60 yards (55m) along an overgrown part of Tinkers Lane. Turn right over a wooden stile, along a well-built stone wall, and up to a metal gate to join the lane to Dinmore House and cottages. Carry on between the buildings and on to a well-kept grassy path.

By August there are some lovely grasses

61

here, and autumn hawkbits, harebells and the lilac flowers of creeping thistle are in bloom on the bank. Thistles are well-known for their attraction to insects, so among the meadow browns and small tortoiseshells, look out for the small skipper. This might be mistaken for a moth, being a small, sturdy butterfly with orange-brown wings. When at rest they sometimes incline the forewings slightly upwards, a characteristic of the skippers.

Via field gates, go up in front of the barn and up the right side of the old monk wall. This is the northern boundary of the Royal Forest of Knaresborough, and here leads the walker up to Burnt Yates. Near this village on the ridge was a gate in the old wall. The name Burnt Yates literally means 'burnt gates'. The first turnpike road from Ripley over Hartwith and Brimham moors had a toll bar by the village inn. But in 1826 a new toll road replaced it to the south, the course taken by the B6165. The village, strung out along the road, has a school (founded in 1760 by Rear Admiral Robert Long), a church with spire, a cricket field and the Bay Horse pub, the latter making a useful lunch stop.

After the last houses and near the village sign, turn right through the red metal gate. Go diagonally across the field, past a lone ash tree, to another gate at the far corner. Turn right on the road for 30 yards (27.5m), then left over a stone stile. Follow the field boundary through three fields, then down the side of a wood, after which the path is down a large field, aiming for the right of Clint Grange Farm. Cross the farm track and, via stiles, join another farm track on the far side of the farm. A ditch

by a concrete bridge has a mass of brooklime growing in it. This blue-flowered marsh plant of the speedwell family has the attractive Latin name of *Veronica beccabunga*. Its shining, fleshy leaves make it look a bit like watercress, and the young leaves have been used in salads and to cure scurvy.

The farm track leads to the village of Clint. The new houses make it look neat and modern, but the village has a long history. Up the road, 100 yards (90m) or so, is the base of an ancient wayside cross with stocks alongside. This corpse cross was where coffin-bearers rested and prayers were said on the way to a burial at Ripley. Further along on the hillside is the site of Clint Hall, the seat of the Beckwith family for over 250 years and, in Elizabethan times, an impressively large mansion. The old village thrived to the end of the eighteenth century, with its own cottage flax industry, the making of yarn and linen, and, like Hampsthwaite, also specialising in the making of spurs. Even in 1820 the population was 412.

From the end of the farm track, the route continues across the road and to the left of the house opposite. The path leads down through the fields, with scattered oaks and ashes, to the road and bridge over the river. The road was widened in 1897, but not the bridge. The three arches date from 1640 when the stone bridge replaced a timber one 'at a cost of £400'. The carriageway has been slightly widened — to 10 feet (3m) — by building out the parapets on each side.

Five minutes' walk returns you to the triangular green in the centre of Hampsthwaite.

WALK 8: HARTWITH AND WINSLEY FROM BIRSTWITH

Start: Birstwith. Grid Ref: 241 595
Distance: 7½ miles (12km)
OS Maps: Pathfinder 653 and 663, or Landranger 99 and 104
Walking Time: 3½ hours

This walk climbs from Birstwith over Swarcliffe Top and Reynards Crag to cross the Nidd near Darley. Rising again on the north side of the valley, over Hartwith Hill, it visits the hamlet of Hartwith and returns through Winsley, with lovely views of the dale. Birstwith lies near the Nidd, north-west of Harrogate, and can be reached from the A59 (Harrogate/Skipton road). There is a small car park in the village.

Birstwith is mentioned in the *Domesday* survey of 1086 as Beristade. It simply means 'farmstead', from *byjar-stathr*, and the community soon became part of Hampsthwaite parish, with a long, quiet history of farming families — that is, until the nineteenth century. The successful cotton king, John Greenwood of Keighley, bought the Swarcliffe estate in 1805, and he and his family created a new look to the village. The Greenwoods replaced the old hall, enlarging it to a stately Victorian mansion, built houses, the new church (completed in 1857), as well as vicarage, school and reading room. Birstwith flourished. It became a parish in its own right, the railway arrived and the first agricultural show was held in 1867.

In 1839 Charlotte Brontë visited Birstwith. Like many Victorian young women, she had taken a post as a governess with a well-to-do family, looking after and teaching the children. In this case it was the Sidgwick family at Lothersdale near Skipton, not a job she particularly enjoyed. On one occasion, the Sidgwicks spent a holiday with their friends the Greenwoods at Swarcliffe Hall. The house had not been extended to its present finery, but was fairly new, large and comfortable. However, Charlotte hated it even more than at Lothersdale. The two families kept up a busy social life, with gatherings and shooting parties and so many visitors that Charlotte, being of a retiring nature, found it very difficult.

Writing early this century, the historian, Harry Speight, described Birstwith as strikingly picturesque:

'Wood and water and luxuriant pasturelands, pleasant country houses with posied gardens are everywhere around, while the stately hall of Swarcliffe, with its fine background of trees high up on the southern hill is a commanding feature of the view.'

Starting from the post office, walk up the road past tall lime trees and St James Church. On the hillside overlooking the dale are the impressive buildings of Swarcliffe Hall, now Grosvenor House School. At the end of the estate wall and the hamlet of Meg Gate, turn right by the open-sided Dutch barn and, at the group of cottages, fork left to go up the field to the brow of the hill. Meg Gate once had the Duke William Inn, village green, maypole and stocks where parish festivities were held. There was even a coalmine nearby which provided small amounts of fuel for local use.

At the brow of the hill, pass through the farmyard and then a stile in the wall on the right. Cross the field to a gate, turning right along the road. This area is known as Swarcliffe Top, from where there are

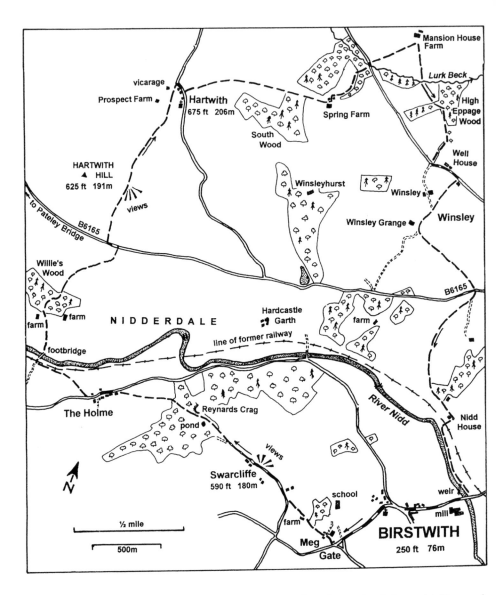

extensive views of Nidderdale. After a
gradual descent along the road, pass
through a red gate, and continue on a grassy
path to the right.

Newly-planted trees and an artificial
pond will help to attract wildlife. Where
the path goes down through a wood, take a

short diversion to the right to visit Reynard
Crag, from which there is a commanding
view of the dale. Notice an angle in the valley as it turns from a south-easterly direction to flow east. Hardcastle Garth, just
across the river, was once a large Quaker
community, and a burial ground lies close

Birstwith is largely a nineteenth century creation. The elegant church of St James was completed in 1857.

by. An old stone cider mill was once worked here.

Return to the woodland path, partly paved with ancient, worn stones, a formerly well-trodden way into the valley. At a small glade full of bracken, turn off to the left to follow field boundaries to the road and the small community of the Holme, an outpost of Darley. The attractive house with a steeply-sloping thatched roof is a reminder of another age.

After the last house, turn off the road to the right across fields to the wooded riverside (the Nidderdale Way), where wild roses, both pink and white, brighten the way. Cross the Nidd by a gracefully-arched footbridge, built on a single steel girder, which supplements an old ford crossing. Smell the aniseed given off by sweet cicely as you brush by, the white masses being one

of the spring-flowering parsleys. There are two others in the same family here, also with white flower-heads, the more delicate cow parsley and — later in the summer — the heavier-looking, but no less attractive, hogweed.

At White Oak Farm, follow the yellow arrows, fork left across the field where horses are kept, and go up the farm drive, passing Willie's Wood on the left. On the side of the lane grow crosswort, greater and lesser stitchwort, and two related pea flowers, bush vetch and meadow vetchling; the former has striking blue flowers in dense spikes with rows of greyish leaflets, while the latter has a cluster of bright yellow flowers and leaflets in pairs.

Turn left at the road for 100 yards (90m), then right through a gate to continue straight up the hill. Looking back across the

65

The tall yet compact pink blooms of the common spotted orchid, which flowers in early July, are to be found on wet ground.

dale is a view of Darley and Holme. You are likely to see the yellowhammer and skylark on these south-facing slopes of Hartwith Hill. The yellowhammer prefers open country with some low cover and few trees.

Like other buntings, it feeds mainly on the ground, but will perch on a wire or bush to deliver its well-known song — a single note *chiz-iz-iz-iz-zeeee*. Bold scribblings on the whitish eggs have given it the name in some areas of 'scribble-lark'. The skylark is only slightly bigger at seven inches (18cm) and pours out its loud song high up in a hovering flight. Though not as handsome as the yellowhammer, its energetic singing has made it a favourite of composers and poets. It nests on the ground and its eggs are off-white to pale green, heavily specked with greenish-brown. In June and again in August, the wall brown butterfly may be seen sunning itself on a stone or bare earth. It is orange-brown with small eyelets or false eyes on the wings.

At the top of the long field, go across to the metal gate and up the middle of the next field, coming out at the vicarage and the hamlet of Hartwith. Turn right to visit Hartwith Church, originally a chapel-of-ease of Kirkby Malzeard and dedicated to St Andrew, but reopened in 1891 as St Judes Church by the Bishop of Richmond. In the churchyard is a sundial, and from here there is a fine view of much of the old Forest of Knaresborough. The name Hartwith means 'stag wood', and is a reminder that both fallow and red deer once roamed here.

Go back to the angle of the road, and take the wooden field gate to roughly follow the line of the wall. Aim for a green field ahead on the hillside that is surrounded by woodland. Pass on the way a solitary oak, a ditch and a wooden stile, skirting the top end of South Wood to arrive at Spring Farm. Around the old farmhouse and farm buildings, swallows and pied wagtails feed on a plentiful supply of insects. Swallows often return, after wintering south of the Sahara, to the same site where they were born, nesting in buildings. By August these graceful fliers, changing direction all the time, gather in large numbers on wires ready for migrating. The pied wagtail also nests around farm buildings and most stay with us all year, though some birds migrate to Europe in the winter.

At Spring House, turn left between two Dutch barns, cross a stile and go down the right side of a sloping field to a gate into the wood on the right. This field is surrounded by woods and a damp patch, about halfway down, is a good flower locality. Common spotted orchid, water mint, changing forget-me-not, ragged robin and marsh ragwort all grow well here. Water mint is the commonest of the mints and, by scattering leaves on the floor, it was once used as a sort of medieval air-freshener. Its flowers form a dense pink spike. The tiny flowers of the pretty changing forget-me-not are yellow at first and later turn to bright blue. If the ground is really wet, keep to the left of the rough stony patch of ground.

From the gate go through the wood, cross the road and bridge over Lurk Beck, and go along the drive to Mansion House Farm. Near the farm, turn right, ford the stream at the bottom of the field, then bear slightly left up the next field to the gate into High Eppage Wood. Rabbits seem to be in abundance. They graze in the field and, when danger threatens, a rabbit warns the others in the colony by thumping with the hind foot. As they scatter, a flash of the white underside of the tail acts as an additional warning.

Go up through the wood, under tall beeches, to another gate at the top. Follow the wall on the left, then pass a line of ash trees to a stile. Keeping to the right edge of the next field and the left of the adjoining one, arrive at the road. This quiet lane was once the turnpike road from Ripley to Brimham, but in the 1820s was replaced by the B6165 further south.

Turn left along the road past Well House, then right before a line of attractive stone cottages. The track leads past Winsley to Winsley Grange. Winsley was recorded in *Domesday Book*, the name originating from an Anglian settlement and meaning 'Wine's clearing', a personal name rather than a reference to the growing of grapes.

Just after Winsley Grange, turn left along the upper edge of two fields to a small kissing gate and a narrow bit of wood. Cross the road and take the drive to Dinmore House, but after 90 yards (80m), turn right onto a path between two fields which is much overgrown with willow, hawthorn, wild roses, blackthorn, foxgloves and bracken. At the bottom of this 'lane', keep straight on, down to a more easily-walked lane, lined in summer with honeysuckle and wild roses. The end of the wood marks the border of the Royal Forest of Knaresborough and the course of the monk wall.

Where the road begins, turn right, past the farm buildings of Nidd House, directly to the riverbank, crossing the line of the old railway. An old boundary stone over to the right says KF-1707, and indicates a corner in the Knaresborough Forest boundary which you have now entered. Turn left down the left bank of the river. There is a fine weir just before the three-arched stone bridge; from here, turn right along Wreaks Road and back into Birstwith.

WALK 9: DARLEY BECK AND THORNTHWAITE

Start: *Dacre Banks. Grid Ref: 197 619*
Distance: *8 miles (12½km)*
OS Maps: *Pathfinder 653, 662 and a small bit of 663. Landranger 99 and 104*
Walking Time: *4 hours*

Starting from Dacre Banks, this walk explores the dale of Darley Beck, one of the small tributary valleys of the Nidd. Though isolated, the area has a long history and the beck's water power attracted several mills. The route includes Darley Mill, Folly Ghyll, Thornthwaite Church and a very old packhorse bridge. Dacre Banks is just across the way from Summerbridge off the B6165 Pateley Bridge road. There is a small car park in the village near the Royal Oak Inn.

Dacre Banks, on the opposite side of the river from Summerbridge and at the foot of the hill from Dacre, makes a useful starting place for a walk. Centred round a triangular green, the village provides the services of a shop, pub, church, car park and garage. Many Nidderdale villages have fine, stone-built bus shelters, but the one in Dacre Banks also has a clock, as well as toilets to the rear.

For many years there was a small school here, founded in 1695 by William Hardcastle, a well-to-do local farmer. The building was then occupied by the youth hostel, one of the first in Yorkshire but now closed. The church was only built in 1837. An old corn mill existed near the river and, in about 1800, a spinning mill was built next to it, being leased to the Ingleson brothers. This was Dacre Banks Mill and was one of the earliest in the dale for the spinning of flax. The single-track Nidd Valley Railway arrived here in 1862, with a station for the village and four passenger trains running daily in each direction.

Starting from the green, go past the Royal Oak Inn and turn left down through the fields to the River Nidd, for a riverside walk of just over a mile (1.8km). (An alternative is to go straight on along the old railway track for a similar distance.) Some of the riverbank is built up against flooding,

and much of it is lined with alders and sycamores while, in normal conditions, the river itself quietly murmurs along in its confined channel. Early in the year, wild garlic, bluebells, broom and gorse provide colour, while blackbirds, wrens and chaffinches add background song.

Over to the right, you may catch sight of the tall chimneys and turreted gables of Low Hall. This is a particularly picturesque old farmhouse with large, stone-mullioned windows. In the eighteenth century it was owned by Robert Benson, ancestor of Dr Benson who became Archbishop of Canterbury and who visited the house in 1892. One of his poems begins:

*'I would live if I had my will
In an old stone grange on a Yorkshire hill
Ivy encircled, lichen streaked,
Grey and mullioned, gable peaked.'*

About a mile along the river are some good stepping stones to a caravan site on the far bank. Turn right here, away from the river, under the old railway bridge. (If you walked along the railway line, leave it here.) Go forward to follow Darley Beck upstream. Just before a footbridge, use the squeezer stile to proceed along the field edge. Keep a look-out for the kingfisher that frequents the tree-lined beck. Go through the farmyard at Low Hurst Farm and, still following the line of the beck,

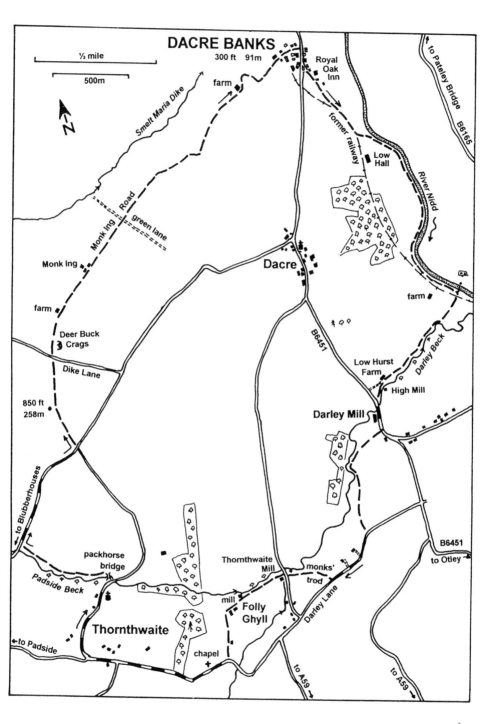

climb to the road. The stepped weir and mill race were built for High Mill, the first of a series of mills along Darley Beck. Some were mills for spinning flax and others for grinding corn.

Turn left at the road to Darley Mill, now a visitor centre and formerly a large corn mill. The mill wheel is still in place to the rear and worth a visit. There was a corn mill on this site as early as the year 1500. Today lots of people visit the mill shop, restaurant and tea garden. Walk up beyond the mill and cottage, and turn right onto a field path signed 'Darley Lane'. In spring, the delicate lilac-pink cuckoo flower grows well in the damp fields. The leaves are edible and make a substitute for watercress. By full summer, near the beck, the large pink flowers of French cranesbill and the deep-red great willowherb appear close together.

Pass a footbridge and soon, following stone stiles, bear away from the beck to reach Darley Lane. Turn right, passing Fog Field House, the name of which refers to the state of a field after the hay has been gathered. Just before a line of cottages, turn right off the road. After a short field, the path bears left towards the beck once more, following the 'monks' trod', where old, worn stones paved the way for monks travelling from Fountains to Bolton Abbey. A wet patch can be bypassed by unusual 'stepping stones' jutting from the wall. The stile to the road is largely hidden by an ash tree opposite Thornthwaite Mill. There are records of linen weaving in Thornthwaite as early as the late sixteenth century. In those days, spinning and weaving were done by hand in the cottages.

Continue straight across the road along a track that leads to the hamlet of Folly Ghyll and along Leeming Lane. The beck is on the right, much smaller now, but still complete with weir and silted outlet to mill-race. Though the mills of Darley Beck were not as large as those on the Nidd, the head of water (or fall in height) was the vital necessity that gave power to the water wheels. Folly Ghyll Mill is the next one to exploit this natural resource.

Turn up the road for just over half a mile (1km), past the Wesleyan chapel and over the brow of the hill, where the upper part of the dale and the scattered hamlet of Thornthwaite come into view. Turn right past the telephone box to Thornthwaite Church.

Built in 1810, the plainly-built church of St Saviours is surrounded by a well-kept, attractive graveyard and stands in a fine position on the valley side. There was once an older chapel here, built about 1402 and dedicated to the little-known St Osyth. The saint is named after a Mercian prince's daughter, murdered by a Viking warrior. The old chapel had a flock of ewes, kept by local farmers, that provided maintenance for the priest.

Go down to Padside Beck and across the quaint packhorse bridge, which could be as old as the fourteenth century. Cross one or two substantial step-stiles to roughly follow the beck up the right side. The path winds between gritstone rocks and overgrown vegetation. Along this wooded stretch of alders, birches and rowan, listen for the songs of warblers and look out for the spotted flycatcher as it swoops for an insect. At the far end of the wall is another fine stile to the road, from which you can see the farms of Padside, the last hamlet in this dale.

Go up the road for 750 yards (700m) to the road junction, and here turn left over the stile. Rather than follow the wheel tracks across this rough grazing land, bear to the right of some gritstone rocks, on a high point, and across to a stile. Ings Farm is to the left and there is a view to Heyshaw Moor. The land here is 800 feet (250m) above sea level, and used for a mixture of

Foxgloves favour woodland and rocky banks, and are a sure sign of summer. The clusters of glove-finger-shaped flowers — aptly named 'finger hat' in German — hang on one side of the stem, forming a mass of pink. The drug digitalis comes from the plant, and its use in testing heart failure was first discovered in 1785.

71

The plainly-built church in Thornthwaite was constructed in 1810, and has attractive surroundings, with its well-tended graveyard and a fine position on the valley side.

sheep and beef-rearing. You may encounter large 'families' of cattle, usually with a big bull among them, though they are not likely to be dangerous or show much interest in you, so long as you pay little attention to them.

Cross the road (Dike Lane) and continue on the farm track past more rocks, called Deer Buck Crags. Pass round the left side of the house and on to Monk Ing. Go through the red gates, between the farm buildings, and along Monk Ing Road. The walled green lane descends into Nidderdale and was once used by monks as they travelled from Fountains Abbey to the outlying granges. There was a grange at Monk Ing itself, and others at Banger House, Fouldshaw and Deer Ing.

Along the lane there are often linnets to be seen, perching on the tops of bushes or on wires. If you manage to get close enough to see this little brown bird, the male has a red forehead and breast, and in summer a chestnut-brown back with grey head. Appropriately, the name comes from *lin*, an old word for flax (hence linen), the seeds of which were considered to be the bird's favourite food. The nearby bushy area of gorse provides good nesting territory.

At the lower end of the lane, follow the finger-post for the Nidderdale Way, straight down the field to a stile near the field corner, then follow the yellow arrows and down through two farms and a snicket back into Dacre Banks village.

WALK 10: BRIMHAM ROCKS FROM SUMMERBRIDGE

Start: Summerbridge. Grid Ref: 202 624
Distance: 7½ miles (12km)
OS Maps: Pathfinder 653 or Landranger 99
Walking Time: 4 hours

This is a lovely walk in and out of woodland, climbing gently to the wonderful rock shapes of Brimham, one of the most popular haunts of the dale, and returning via some of the historical old farmhouses of Hartwith. Summerbridge lies on the B6165 from Ripley to Pateley Bridge, and at the junction of the B6451 from Otley. There is space for a few cars on a wide part of the main road.

Until the 1820s Summerbridge, as a community, hardly existed — just a mill and one or two cottages. Then two events prompted the growth of the nineteenth-century industrial village. In 1825, New York Mill was built next to the River Nidd, where it made use of water power for the spinning of flax. The large mill provided employment for a good number of workers and Summerbridge was but a few minutes' walk away. By 1828 the new turnpike road was ready for use, providing an essential transport line for the growing industry and a focus for the new village. Summerbridge also acquired two further mills, an iron foundry which made fireplaces and machine parts, a ropeworks, school and Wesleyan chapel.

A bridge has existed here at least since the mid-fifteenth century, when 'Summer-brig' was mentioned in the bursar's books of Fountains Abbey, and was being used by monks going to and from the granges on the south side of the river at Dacre, Monk Ing and Heyshaw. The present bridge has two arches, has been widened to double its original width, and probably dates from the seventeenth century.

Today, Summerbridge is a residential village, particularly well-served by a post office, an unusually good variety of shops and the Flying Dutchman Inn, and there

is a large sawmill and timber yard by the river. Small industry keeps New York Mill as a going concern, though there are plans to convert it to luxury homes.

From the Flying Dutchman, a pub named after the racehorse that won both the Derby and the St Leger in 1849, proceed up Hartwith Bank, past the footpath to Stripe Lane (the return route); further up, turn off on a track to the left, labelled 'Old Spring Wood'. The path goes along the lower part of this broad-leaved woodland, where oak, sycamore and beech attract woodland birds and where, in spring, among the chorus of chaffinches, wrens and bluetits, you should hear the melodious songs of the willow warbler and blackcap. The agile grey squirrel is fairly common, active by day and easy to watch. It builds its nest, or dray, of twigs and leaves in the fork of a tree. Summer drays are often high in the branches, while the more substantial winter dray is built on a strong branch near the trunk.

From the wood, go through the wooden gate on to a short green lane past a beautifully-built barn, dated 1784. Across the way is a pair of old gateposts carved, like many in the area, for the insertion of three horizontal bars. Pass a duck pond and house, and continue along the lower edge of the wood, with a view of the valley to the left.

The snipe, with its long bill and attractively-patterned plumage, seldom allows close approach. It is most active in the morning and evening, but you may flush one as it calls out and flies away in a low zigzag. They breed on Brimham Moor.

The old hedge contains blackthorn, hazel, willow and holly. About 100 yards (90m) before the next stone-built farmhouse, turn off to the right through the birch trees, then straight across a field to the road.

Turn left along the road for about 130 yards (120m). Over to the left is Braisty Woods, a thriving little community of farms and cottages. Originally a grange of Fountains Abbey, the farm was rebuilt by the Skaife family in the early seventeenth century and became the centre of a small tanning industry. In 1825 William Hebden lived there when he built New York Mill.

Just after the bend in the road, turn right over a low wall and, bearing slightly left, cross the field, to find a stile amid a thicket of blackthorn. Go straight on to join the path that comes up from Smelthouses. Continue up the hill, across a clearing where Brimham Rocks come into view, and continue through the margin of High Wood as far as the road.

Holly bushes, just into the clearing, attract the dainty holly blue butterfly. This is a speciality of Nidderdale, being rare elsewhere in Yorkshire. The caterpillars feed on holly flower buds in the spring, but the second brood in the autumn needs ivy for its food plant, so holly and ivy together are a vital part of the life cycle. The butterfly is rather like the common blue, but the undersides of the wings are pale blue, unlike the common blue which are brown. You may see orange tip butterflies here too, on the wing at the same time, usually in May. Another small butterfly is the green hairstreak, which you may see higher up among the rocks. When settled with wings folded, the metallic green is striking but it also makes a good camouflage, especially among the bilberry on which it lays its eggs.

At the road, turn left for a short way to the entrance of Brimham Rocks. Go up the small path from the notice board, at the far corner of the car park, for an impressive

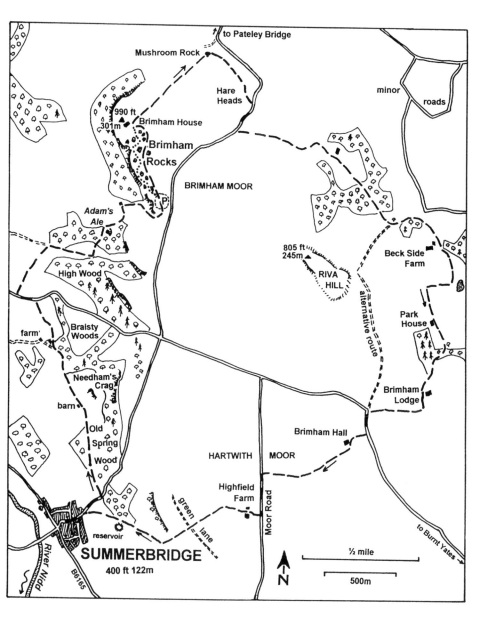

scenic walk among the many rock formations to reach Brimham House, from where there is a wonderful view. The groups of rocks stand tall and rugged in a variety of fantastic shapes and structures, and many have been given names such as Sphinx, Camel, Lover's Leap and Dancing Bear.

Brimham Rocks have been attracting tourists for over 200 years. In the year 1792, Lord Grantley built a house here 'for the accommodation of persons whose curiosity might prompt them to visit this world of wonders', a time when the rocks were described as 'druidical monuments' and when a little sculpturing was quite in order to improve the shapes. The building is now a visitor centre and, since 1979, the 387 acre (155ha) estate has been under the care of the National Trust, who have put into operation a long-term conservation plan, including improved facilities for visitors. Most of the area has been made a Site of Special Scientific Interest. From the trig point to the rear of the centre, there are extensive views.

From Brimham House, go up to the right of the kiosk, cross the bigger, north-south path and continue eastwards to some

A gatepost near Summerbridge with slots carved out for fitting three horizontal bars.

rock slabs, partly covered in heather and bilberry. The path divides round these and joins up again, bringing the Mushroom Rock into view. From the track and from the Mushroom Rock there are panoramic views: to the north-west is the hump of Great Whernside, and on a clear day Penhill in Wensleydale is visible on the horizon; to the north-east are the Cleveland Hills and the industries of Teesmouth; while eastwards, across the Vale of York, you should be able to see the White Horse of Kilburn on the southern slopes of the Hambleton Hills.

Brimham is the home of several moorland birds. The red grouse is usually about, warning you to *go bak, go bak bak bak*; the curlew, skylark and snipe all breed in the area, and are likely to heard or seen.

From the Mushroom Rock, turn right to find small tracks through the heather to the rocks of Hare Heads, which form a large variety of rock shapes, well worth exploring, and where few visitors penetrate. From the last of these, drop down to the Summerbridge road. Turn right along the road, then left along a concrete farm track.

The track leads to Summer Wood House, beyond which, pass down a field by a line of hawthorn and blackthorn and into a wood. The path skirts the end of Riva Hill, and passes between the farmland of Shepherd's Lodge and Brimham Lodge. The latter, a lodge of Fountains Abbey, was rebuilt in 1661 by Thomas Braithwaite; today it is an impressive farmhouse.

Join the road for 150 yards (140m), then turn right to Brimham Hall, passing round the left side of the house. The hall was formerly the principal residence of the estate, built on the site of a grange and chapel of Fountains Abbey. There are still traces of inscriptions on stones and of monastic fishponds on the left of the house as you go by. The building was rebuilt in a simpler style in the eighteenth century.

76

Brimham Hall is on the site of a grange and chapel of Fountains Abbey, though the present structure dates from rebuilding in the eighteenth century.

Cross the beck and follow the wall up the hill, turning left onto Moor Road. From this ridge on Hartwith Moor, some 750ft (225m) above sea level, there are broad views across to the plain of York. After 300 yards (280m), go up the driveway to Highfield Farm, passing round the right side of the house and immediate farm buildings, and up through a new small plantation.

Keep near the wall on the left, and soon cross a green lane (from Brimham to Edge Nook) and enter along another, bordered with stout walls of millstone grit. Among the flowers are violets, wood sorrel, foxglove, greater stitchwort and wild strawberry; ahead is a fine view of Nidderdale,

with Dacre Banks standing out on the far side of the valley.

Where the lane bears right is a gorse-covered hillside. The willow warbler seems to like the scattered trees and shrubs and, with binoculars and a little patience, you should be able to get a good view of this stalwart summer visitor. The adult birds are olive-brown, but if you see the young fledglings in June or July they have quite a yellowish look to them, not at all like their parents.

Pass an underground reservoir and drop down opposite a rocky bluff, along a line of oaks and bird cherry, then follow a narrow path between the houses and into Summerbridge.

WALK 11: HAWKSHAW GILL WOOD AND HEYSHAW MOOR

Start: *Dacre Banks. Grid Ref: 197 619*
Distance: *5 miles (8km)*
OS Maps: *Pathfinder 652 or Landranger 99*
Walking Time: *2½ hours*

Peaceful woods, moors and meadows make up most of this walk from Dacre Banks. A steady climb of 550 feet (170m) brings you from Lead Wath Wood up to High Hood Gap and the edge of Heyshaw Moor. From the hamlet of Heyshaw, the route descends through fields and North Wood back to the start. There are some fine views, and the walk is good for observing a wide variety of birds. There is a useful car park near the Royal Oak Inn at Dacre Banks. The village is on the B6451 from Otley and just across the river from Summerbridge.

Dacre Banks makes a good starting point for walkers, as not only is there a free car park and a pub with an interesting and original menu, but there is also a good general village store and public toilets.

From the triangular village green and its fine young oak tree, go down the road past the shop, to take the footpath that leads from Cabin Lane, signed 'Glasshouses'. Pass the church on the right, and then rocky outcrops of millstone grit and the site of an old quarry on the left. The track soon crosses the line of the former railway, to run alongside it for about a third of a mile (530m). The Nidderdale Railway was a single line that opened to Pateley Bridge on the 1st May 1862, and Dacre Banks had its own station. The last train ran in 1964 and the track was lifted a year later.

Near the entrance of Lead Wath Wood, turn up the forest road for a quiet stroll through attractive woodland. Originally planted by the Forestry Commission in the early 1960s, the wood is now privately owned. Walkers are welcome and will enjoy this interesting stretch of woodland and its wildlife. Although mainly spruce and larch, the wood is light and open, not too over-bearing and contains a few broad-leaved trees.

The wood attracts a wide variety of birds. Pheasants are bred here and are likely to be seen on any visit. In summer, when seed is put down for the young pheasants along the track, this is also a general invitation to jays, chaffinches and grey squirrels to partake of the feast. The jay is a common bird, but so secretive that it is difficult to get a good view of it. When you do, the colours are striking. The body is buff-coloured with a white rump, a distinctive bright blue wing-patch and a streaked crest. It is not the birdwatcher's favourite, as it steals nestlings and eggs of other birds such as thrushes and blackbirds. With so many small birds about, the woods and open glades make an ideal habitat for the fierce-looking sparrowhawk. This fast-moving, low-flying hunter may be seen on any part of the walk. Grey above and pale beneath, the sparrowhawk will dash along one side of a wall or hedge and flick over to the other side to take its prey by surprise.

Follow the broad forest road, past a duck pond, left at a hut, gradually winding up the hill, forking left again and up to a gate at the top. Along the edge of the path grow selfheal and eybright, two plants (in bloom in July and August) which have been widely used for the cure of ailments. Eyebright is a whitish flower, which on close inspection has two lips decorated with a yellow spot

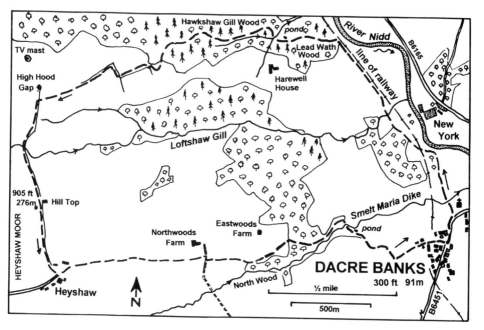

and purple lines. An extract from the plant is still used in eye lotions. Selfheal, with the attractive Latin name of *Prunella*, has a compact head of small purple flowers and was once thought to be a cure for wounds and sore throats.

From the gate at the upper end of the wood, the path curves round to the right, then follows the blackened gritstone walls, roughly aiming for the TV mast, up to High Hood Gap. The house of this name is on the right, and straight ahead is a large area of old quarries, the mounds of waste now clad in heather and bilberry. The quarries once produced a high-quality building stone. Beyond the quarry is the survey pillar of High Crag Ridge, at 1,085 feet (331m) above sea level.

Turn left along the track for just under a mile (1.2km), passing Hill Top, the highest point on the walk, and on to Heyshaw. To the left is a view across the valley to Brimham Rocks on the other horizon and down Nidderdale; on the right is Heyshaw

Moor, with broad stretches of heather and resident grouse, meadow pipit and cuckoo. Along the track-side, among the heather, grow cross-leaved heath, crowberry and hard fern.

Heyshaw is a small hamlet of houses, farms and cottages where stone-mullioned windows and decorative finials give the buildings an old and attractive image. The name is mentioned in the *Domesday* survey of 1086 and, soon after, the monks of Fountains established a grange which may have been in use as a summer farm. But 1,000 years earlier the Romans were transporting lead through here from the mines of Greenhow to their base at Boroughbridge. Just how the heavy ingots were lost is left to the imagination, but in 1734 two large pigs of lead were found near Heyshaw, buried two feet deep at the side of a track. They each weigh 155lbs (70kg), measure 23 by 5¾ inches (59x14cm) and date from AD 81. One of them can be seen at Ripley Castle and the other is in the British Museum.

The cowslip's Latin name of primula *means 'first rose' and refers to the plant's early flowering. The cowslip is said to have sprung from the post where St Peter dropped the keys to Heaven — so the flowers resemble a bunch of keys.*

From Heyshaw, instead of taking the Nidderdale Way, go through the gate and straight down the fields. The first step-stile is midway between two field gates and, as you get near Northwoods Farm (on the left), turn right onto a lane for a few paces, then left through two fields to a gate. Cross the track to Eastwoods Farm, go alongside some woodland and then, from a group of ash trees, bear half-left to the corner of the field and a gate that leads into part of North Wood.

Here is a lovely woodland path that descends through silver birches and bluebells, with a scenic little stream on the right named Smelt Maria Dike — an allusion to lead-smelting with a twist in the name from the original 'smeltmire'. In May, among the chirpings of the chaffinches, blackbirds and thrushes, you should hear the bright songs of the blackcap and willow warbler.

In the autumn of 1994, a fungus foray in North Wood produced an amazing 109 species of fungi. Among them were some of the colourful specimens illustrated on page 27 — honey fungus, bay bolete, fly agaric and false chanterelle. The great number and wide variety of species gives some indication of the age and complexity of this mixed woodland.

At the bottom of the wood, turn right along the track. After fording the beck, there is a rather unkempt area on the left with a pond where coltsfoot, teasel, ragwort and hedge bindweed have all colonised mounds of earth. The lovely yellow coltsfoot is one of the first flowers of the year; later, the hoof-shaped leaves grow to eight inches across (20cm). Ragwort is another yellow flower on taller, branching stems flowering from May onwards, and the creeping hedge bindweed has pure white blooms. The seed-eating goldfinch feeds on thistle heads but, by autumn, they are attracted to the teasel, being the only bird able to extract the nutritious seeds from this plant.

Follow the track past the farm, from where Summerbridge comes into view across the dale, and, after crossing a ditch, take the direct path down to the left, through field and farm, to Dacre Banks.

WALK 12: BRIMHAM ROCKS FROM GLASSHOUSES

Start: Glasshouses. Grid Ref: 173 645
Distance: 7½ miles (12km)
OS Maps: Pathfinder 652 and 653 or Landranger 99
Walking Time: 4 hours

This delightful walk holds more variety than most. From Glasshouses it proceeds along the river to Low Laithe, then gently climbs through woodland to the hamlet of Smelthouses and more woods to Brimham. It continues among the famous, towering rocks, picks up a flavour of heather moorland before descending by the wooded Fell Beck. The last part of the walk has fine, open views across the dale as it returns to Glasshouses. The village is just off the B6165 a mile south of Pateley Bridge. There is limited parking near the green or lower down the hill near the school.

Glasshouses is built on a terminal moraine of the Nidderdale Glacier. The name is an old one that suggests glass was made here, perhaps for one of the abbeys. There have been a few farms and cottages here in the years since, but the present village dates from the nineteenth century. The flax-spinning mill was built in 1812 and, first as tenants and then as owners, the Metcalfe brothers, John and George, extended the mill so that by mid-century it employed 264 workers, mostly women and girls. Men took the part of mechanics and overlookers.

Work in the mill was hard, and started at six o'clock in the morning until seven in the evening, for a seventy-two hour week. Girls of eight or ten earned two shillings (10p) a week employed as 'doffers' — taking the full bobbins from the spinning frames and replacing them with empty ones — while their mothers, as spinners, took home six shillings. Occasionally, children who sat down or were too slow could be given a stripe or two by the overlooker, who carried a leather strap. There was a forty minute dinner-break, though spinners had to take breakfast or a mug of tea while watching their machines. Seven days' holiday without pay was given during the year, including at least one day in September for Pateley Feast. The weaving of linen was still mostly carried out on cottage hand-looms in the dale.

Walk down towards the river and then through the mill yard, past the clock and round to the right of the buildings for the riverside footpath. The textile mill closed twenty years ago, but the impressive buildings now house a selection of small businesses. One of these is a winery which occupies the cellars where, in the tasting room, it is possible to sample elderflower, gooseberry and other fruit wines.

The path to Low Laithe hugs the riverbank for most of the way. To start with, the river is narrow, dark and deep, full of secrets and brown trout. Alders line the bank and, where the path takes to the field edge, the river widens and flows faster. The high right bank and the shelf of land to the left are river terraces, remnants of a former floodplain, indicating how the river has cut down into its old bed.

Pass under the arch of the former railway. There is plenty of vegetation cover for small birds here; the long-tailed tit, often in the company of bluetits and great tits, makes good use of it. If it weren't for the long tail which makes up half its length, this tiny bird would be the smallest British bird. It spends two months making a neat, oval, ball-shaped nest, lined with spiders'

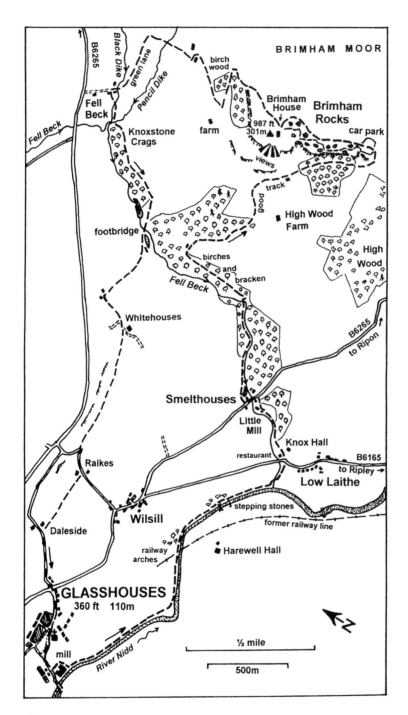

BRIMHAM MOOR

B6265

Black Dike

green lane

Pencil Dike

birch
wood

Fell Beck

Fell
Beck

Knoxstone
Crags

farm

Brimham
House

987 ft
301m

views

Brimham
Rocks

car park

track

bog

High Wood
Farm

footbridge

birches

and

Fell Beck

bracken

High
Wood

B6265
to Ripon

Whitehouses

Smelthouses

Little
Mill

Knox Hall

restaurant

B6165
to Ripley →

Raikes

Low Laithe

Daleside

Wilsill

stepping stones

former railway line

railway
arches

Harewell Hall

GLASSHOUSES
360 ft   110m

mill

River Nidd

½ mile

500m

webs. The nest is so small that the bird has a folding device at the base of its tail to enable it to enter. These delightful birds may be seen at any time of year, as they don't stray far from where they were born.

Cross a side stream, and pass a wooden footbridge and old stepping stones. Across the river is Harewell Hall where, over three centuries, families of Luptons, Carrs and Simpsons have lived. On the river, mallard and grey wagtail stay close to the water. The long tail and yellow underparts of the slender grey wagtail help to identify it and, though a resident, in winter it may move to wet places lower down the valley.

Turn up the side stream of Fell Beck, to cross it on a small footbridge and up to the road at Low Laithe. The old mill is now a restaurant and Knox Hall stands on the hillside. The path still follows the beck, crosses the road, and passes in and out of woodland past Little Mill (which was once the scene of flax-spinning, then bobbin-making) to Smelthouses. Here the monks of

The long-tailed tit is the most sedentary of all British birds, and doesn't move more than a mile or so from its nest.

A female yellowhammer with her young. The yellowhammer is a resident farmland bird, where it will take up a perch in a tree along the hedgerows to deliver its song of high notes ending in a drawn-out chweee *('little-bit-of-bread-and-no-cheese'). In winter you may see them feeding in the stubble and ploughed fields.*

Fountains Abbey smelted lead ore brought from their mines at Greenhow, and in 1795 the Kirkby family built the earliest flax-spinning mill in Nidderdale on the side of Fell Beck.

Turn left over the bridge and right, signed 'Whitehouses' and the Nidderdale Way. The solid and impressive wall on the left supported the mill race, which the path follows for a short way.

The beck flows in a steep-sided, wooded ravine, where there is a wide variety of wild flowers. Among bluebells, greater stitch-wort, wood sorrel and wild garlic, there are the creamy flowers and delicate foliage of

climbing corydalis, and larger plants of sweet cicely and foxglove.

Cross the wooden footbridge and turn up the far bank, with a sharp left after fifty yards (45m) through birches and bracken. Turn up to the right in front of a house along a good track, looping round and steadily climbing the escarpment until the sculptured rocks of Brimham come into view. There are quite a few holly bushes on the way which, in May, are frequented by the lovely holly blue butterfly.

Keep bearing left to the car park, and take the small gravel path that starts at the notice board. Even in quiet times of the year

The Dancing Bear at Brimham Rocks. The formation of Brimham Rocks, in the Kinderscout Grit, has been due to the presence of strong joints between the stacks, along which weathering and erosion have taken place, leaving one lot of rocks separate from another. They have been a tourist attraction for 200 years.

there are usually a few visitors to Brimham, which has become one of the most popular tourist attractions in the Dales. Families with children, aspiring young rock climbers and their instructors, ramblers and sightseers, the elderly and infirm all find some interest, excitement or sense of discovery among the many weird and wonderful rocks, with the ever-present wide views of Nidderdale.

Some of the weird and fantastic shapes to be seen at Brimham Rocks.

From Brimham House, the route needs detailed directions. Go up to the right of the refreshment kiosk on a small path, turn left and descend to a farm track. Turn left along the track and, fifty yards (45m) after leaving a birch wood, strike backward (to the right) through a field gate with a stone wall on the left, making for a group of farm buildings at North Pasture. Go round the right side of the farmhouse, through a metal gate (on the left), then follow a line of telegraph poles to join a green lane down the hill, to a group of cottages at Fell Beck.

Turn left round the last cottage and cross the field. Black Dike and Pencil Dike enter Fell Beck near here, but at the entrance to the wood, turn sharply up to the left to some rocks known as Knoxstone Crags, then right to enter the wood along

its upper edge. On leaving the wood, the path then descends to a new footbridge, proceeds for a few paces up a lane, turns left, then leaves the track to cross fields to the right. Follow the arrows to climb out of the valley of Fell Beck for extensive views to the south and the 'golf balls' of Menwith Hill. At the cottages, turn left to Whitehouses. Here, go straight across and through the gate opposite for a fine walk below a steep rocky scarp. The slopes are covered with gorse bushes, bilberry and heather, then bracken and brambles. The views are across Nidderdale to Guisecliff, topped by the television mast.

At the road, turn down for 180 yards (165m), then right through a gate 'to Raikes Farm'. Go through the fields and down the minor road to return to Glasshouses.

WALK 13: PANORAMA WALK AND SCOTGATE ASH

Start: *Pateley Bridge. Grid Ref: 158 656*
Distance: *3 miles (5km)*
OS Maps: *Pathfinder 652 or Landranger 99*
Walking Time: *1½ to 2 hours*

This short walk from Pateley Bridge involves a steep climb to the ruins of the old church, wonderful views of the dale from the popular Panorama Walk, a visit to the old quarries of Scotgate Ash and an even steeper descent down the Incline. This is the former quarry winding track where there is a need for grippy footwear. The walk makes a good introduction to the area and, on a fine day, the stiff uphill start is worth it for the extensive panorama. There are car parks in Pateley Bridge off High Street and along Nidd Walk by the river.

The first mention of Pateley Bridge is in the twelfth century. Written in those days as 'Patheleybrigg', the meaning becomes 'the bridge by the forest clearing near the paths' (rather than of the 'pate' or badger).

The 'paths' are old monastic routes, one across the dale from Fountains to Grassington, and another linking granges along the dale. A Tuesday market was granted in 1320, with a fair on the Feast of St Mary in

Pateley Bridge. St Cuthberts Church stands at the top of the street, and on the left is St Cuthberts Primary School, built by the Metcalfe family in the Scottish Baronial style. Between them is the musuem.

87

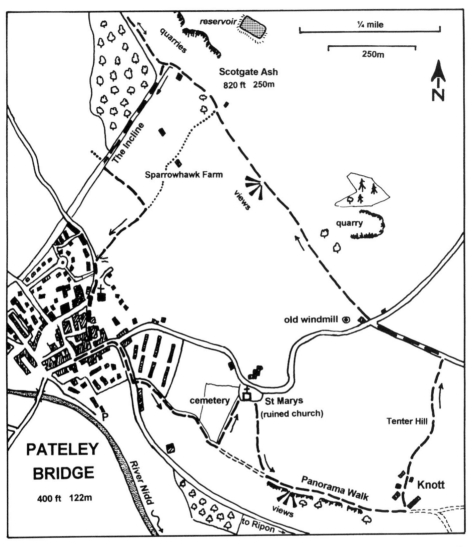

September. Today the market is a Saturday livestock sale, and the Nidderdale Show, in the second half of September, is still an important annual event, known for most of its history as Pateley Feast.

The 1794 survey of agriculture in the West Riding described Pateley as:

'a thriving place . . . the inhabitants were in no danger of starving for want of butcher's meat. A great deal of linen is manufactured in this place. Much butter is salted here and sent to York for the London market.'

Lean hams, with not enough fat on them for local tastes, were also sent to London, and pork went to Lancashire.

In the nineteenth century, leadmining and quarrying brought further prosperity.

The arrival of the railway in 1862 helped to give another boost to trade, when high-quality flagstone and building stone soon became an important export, and tourists also flocked up the dale. The Incline from Scotgate Ash, built in 1871, boosted the quarrying trade.

Much of the town is solidly built of the local stone, which each summer now is enhanced by the colourful displays of hanging baskets and floral window boxes. In this friendly town, there is plenty to interest visitors: the Nidderdale Museum, King Street Workshops, Recreation Centre, and a good range of shops, pubs, cafés and restaurants. Pateley Bridge is the ideal centre to explore the many miles of Nidderdale footpaths.

Start the walk by going up High Street and round on to the Ripon road. Just past the Methodist church, take the steps up to the left, signed 'Panorama Walk'. At the top of this steep ginnel is the cemetery. Keep on up the hill a little further, to take the narrow walled path on the left that runs above the cemetery to the old church ruins.

St Marys was first mentioned in 1321 as a chantry chapel of Ripon parish, and in 1580 the curate, Thomas Briggs, was committed to York Castle for being too Catholic in his outlook. The ruined buildings date from the late seventeenth century, and the church was certainly beautifully situated, with a magnificent view of the valley below. In 1780, John Wesley preached here, when the small Methodist chapel could not hold the large congregation. The roof has gone, but the walls and tower remain reasonably intact. The new Church of St Cuthbert, in the upper town, replaced this one in 1826 (with a Parliamentary grant and a new patron saint) after which, at least, churchgoers did not have to struggle so far up the hill each Sunday.

Birdwatchers may well have noticed the presence of goldfinches on the way up, and might catch sight of a bullfinch around the old ruin. This secretive bird is blue-grey above and pinkish below, with a white wing patch and bold white rump. It has been well-described as portly and neckless.

From the church, take the kissing gate that leads across two fields to rejoin Panorama Walk. A jutting rock on the right with a protective railing affords a wonderful view down into the valley below and across to Guisecliff and Yorke's Folly.

Along the pathside, among vetch, speedwell and stitchwort, grows cow parsley, known as keck or kex in Yorkshire. This common member of the parsley family also goes by the descriptive name of Queen Anne's lace, grows two to three feet (60-90cm) in height and has a delicate head of white florets.

At the hamlet of Knott, turn left past the stone cottages, the last one of which has stone-mullioned windows and a barn adjoining. The walled path climbs steadily up Tenter Hill, a tell-tale name of textile days when linen, after washing and bleaching, was stretched out on tenterhooks to dry.

Turn left along the tarred road and, at the t-junction, go straight on over the stile and past the stone tower of a former windmill. When it was working during the nineteenth century, the windmill had iron sails and contained machinery which powered the polishing of stone slabs destined for parts of London such as Euston Station.

Join the lane that leads to Scotgate Ash. From here there are brilliant views of Pateley Bridge, 400 feet (120m) below. The quarries are now quiet and scenic, and a haven for wildlife. Many of the rocks have interesting geological structures such as ripple marks, worm casts and cross-bedding *(see the photographs on page 3)*.

With the arrival of the railway, the transport of heavy goods became relatively cheap. It was George Metcalfe who had

89

Cottages in the tiny hamlet of Knott, above Pateley Bridge.

done much to persuade the railway company to extend the line to Pateley, and he went on to develop the quarrying of stone at Scotgate Ash, building the Incline to take stone down to the railway sidings in the town. George Metcalfe built cottages on Millfield Street for his quarry workers and, in 1872, he set up a Quarry Club to look after their medical welfare.

The stone was some of the best in the country, especially the large slabs of flagstone and sandstone for building. The biggest slabs, up to fifteen feet (4.5m) long, were especially useful for paving dockside quays (including those at Hull), railway platforms and steps of large buildings. The medium-grained micaceous sandstone was used to build the National Gallery and the museums of South Kensington in London, York Art Gallery and many other public buildings throughout the country, and, of course, much of Pateley Bridge itself.

You can explore further along the path, returning to the top of the Incline which is next to Scotgate Cottage. Descend steeply until about halfway down the Incline, then turn left via a stile and fields, to continue down the hill on the track from Sparrow Hawk Farm to return, past the parish church, to the town centre.

WALK 14: GUISECLIFF CRAGS AND TWO STOOPS

Start: Pateley Bridge. Grid Ref: 158 656
Distance: 5 miles (8km)
OS Maps: Pathfinder 652 or Landranger 99
Walking Time: 2½ to 3 hours

Here is a lovely walk with constant changes of scenery. Starting from Pateley Bridge, it takes the well-trodden path along the river to Glasshouses, climbs through Guisecliff Woods via the tarn, to reach the craggy cliff-top high above the dale. It continues along the edge of heather moors, visits Two Stoops (or Yorke's Folly) and the Crocodile Rock, then descends through the nature reserve of Skrikes Wood and ends with a stroll through Bewerley village. The cliff top is dangerous, especially for young children, as there are abrupt crevasses near the path and the cliff has an unprotected edge with a vertical drop of a hundred feet or more. There is good parking space near the river in Pateley Bridge.

In the early sixteenth century, Leland records that Pateley Bridge was 'of wood'. The present stone bridge probably dates from the mid-eighteenth century, when two new turnpike roads, one from Ripon and one from Knaresborough, met at Pateley Bridge *en route* to Grassington and Skipton, and boosted the market and trade of the town.

This was the time when the flax industry first spread up the dale. At first flax was hand-spun but, by the 1790s, machinery was introduced for spinning, and linen-weaving was carried on as a cottage industry. George and Elizabeth Metcalfe built up a flax-dressing and spinning business (in addition to their brewery, inn and farm) and, as described by Bernard Jennings in *A History of Nidderdale*, 'Elizabeth Metcalfe used to ride to Hull to buy Baltic flax, which was heckled (or combed) in a flax-dressing shop in Pateley Bridge, put out to spinners and sold as yarn'.

From the bridge, go along Nidd Walk and the left bank of the river, following it for just over a mile (1.8km) downstream to Glasshouses. It is a popular footpath, much of it on the raised riverbank lined with alders. The line of the former railway up to Pateley runs through fields to the left. Pass

a weir, where machinery to work the sluice is still in position and where, across the iron bridge, stands Castlestead, the mansion of George Metcalfe junior. In the nineteenth century, the Metcalfe family further developed their brewing, quarrying and flax industries in the area. Continue between the mill-race and Glasshouses Dam, the large millpond that once turned a thirty-two foot (9.75m) waterwheel, which powered the machinery of the Metcalfe's flax-spinning mill in the village. The mill dam is now the scene of canoeing lessons for young people, and is inhabited by coots. In the spring, the rhododendrons are a colourful sight.

Turn right over the tubular steel bridge, up and away from the river, and right again in front of a row of cottages. The track leads past Hollin House Farm and Bobbin Mill Cottage, complete with millpond. Enter Guisecliff Woods, where a small path winds up through the trees. The woods are deciduous with a variety of trees, such as oak, birch and sycamore, with undergrowth of holly and honeysuckle.

Turn left on to a bigger track and then, at a grassy triangular junction, keep right to continue steeply uphill. Where the path veers to the left, leave the main path and

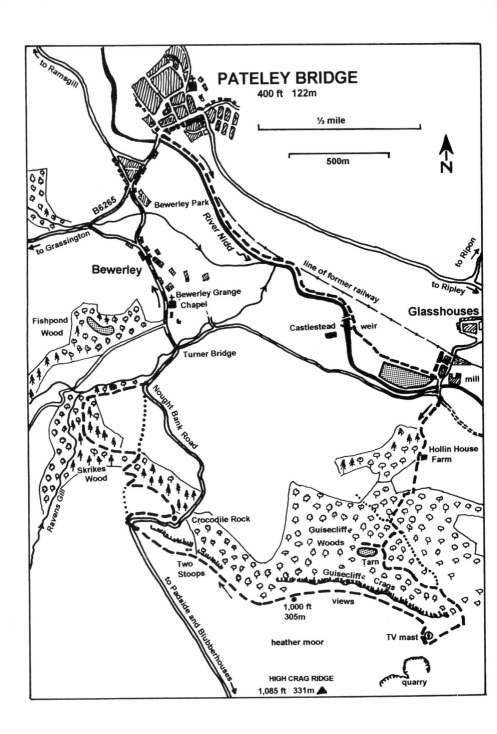

Guisecliff Tarn, near Pateley Bridge, is a haven for birdlife. The tarn, which has a rough path all round, is overlooked by Guisecliff Crags.

look out for the tarn beyond some enormous rocks. You could easily miss it. Guisecliff Tarn is a peaceful, idyllic spot and you may catch sight of the rocky heights reflected in the water. It is possible to walk all round the small lake. In spring and early summer, tune in to the birdsong and, among the robins and blackbirds, you will probably hear the clear song of the blackcap and the descending notes of the willow warbler. I was lucky enough to see a tree pipit parachute to a topmost branch and continue to call heartily.

Return to the track up through the woods. The area is part of a large landslip that occurred a few thousand years ago (soon after the Ice Age). The slopes are scattered with angular rocks and boulders, many of which are grown over by bilberry and heather. On coming out of the trees,

curve up to the right and follow the stone wall up to the TV mast. There are extensive views along Nidderdale, and you should be able to make out Glasshouses, Wilsill, Low Laithe, Brimham Rocks and Summerbridge.

Turn right (round the back of the mast) for an amazing walk along the top of Guisecliff Crags, with superb views of the dale below. The path winds among abrupt and deep crevasses in the gritstone, where the original joint system has been widened by erosion. Take great care where you tread, as some of the narrow fissures can become covered over by bracken fronds and are particularly dangerous. At one of the viewpoints you can see the small tarn 250 feet (75m) below among the treetops, while birch, rowan and oak cling to the cliffs.

From the ladder stile, there is an open

Yorke's Folly overlooks Pateley Bridge, and is known locally as Two Stoops.

view of extensive and uninterrupted heather moorland to the left — a glorious sight in August when the purple heather is in full bloom — culminating in High Crag Ridge, with its survey column at 1,085 feet (331m). On the right, the view is obscured by a six foot wall.

The next ladder stile brings you to Yorke's Folly, known locally as 'Two Stoops' and built to look like an old ruin. There used to be three, but one of them collapsed in a storm 100 years ago. They were built in this prominent position in the late eighteenth century by John Yorke of Bewerley Hall, partly to provide employment during bad times; for their efforts, workmen were paid fourpence a day and a loaf of bread. The rocks and cliffs are the haunt of the kestrel, so keep an eye open for this hovering falcon with an orange

brown back. In summer the cuckoo —much the same size as the kestrel and very hawk-like in flight — inhabits the edge of the moor, making use of meadow pipits' nests in which to lay its eggs. There are magnificent views of Pateley Bridge and upper Nidderdale from here.

Take the diagonal path down to a sharp bend in the road. Cross the road and turn right through the heather to visit the Crocodile Rock. You can sit in the croc's mouth for shelter! Descend above the wood and rejoin the main footpath.

Enter Skrikes Wood, a nature reserve and a particularly beautiful stretch of woodland, rich in plant and birdlife. Descend to a stile, and turn left for a delightful path through silver birches, then conifers, more birches and some lovely beeches. Reaching the beck — this is the lower part of Raven's Gill — follow it down to a stile, by which grow the delicate flowers of wood stitchwort; a flowery bank on the right has violets, herb robert and tall foxgloves.

At the road, turn down to the stone bridge, known as Turner Bridge, and left through the *Domesday* village of Bewerley back to Pateley Bridge. On the right is the small and peaceful Bewerley Grange Chapel, built in 1494 and restored in 1965. It was built by Marmaduke Huby, one of the last abbots of Fountains Abbey, and his initials and motto are on the east wall. Bewerley Hall was the residence of the Yorke family until the 1920s, when the house was dismantled and the estate sold. The park is now used as an outdoor education centre for the county, and is the venue for the Nidderdale Agricultural Society's annual show.

Pass Bewerley's village green, and follow the roadside footpath to return to Pateley Bridge. All along the walls grow the little purple flowers of ivy-leaved toadflax, together with the ferns, maidenhair spleenwort and wall rue.

Stoats live in hedges and woods. About twelve inches (30cm) long, this slim, pale brown carnivore has reddish-brown fur with creamy-white underparts, and a distinctive black tip to its four inch (11cm) tail.

WALK 15: ASHFOLD SIDE, THE LEADMINES AND GREENHOW HILL

Start: *Pateley Bridge. Grid Ref: 158 656*
Distance: *8½ miles (13½km)*
OS Maps: *Pathfinder 652 or Landranger 99*
Walking Time: *4½ hours*

Here is a walk through mining and quarrying country, with many reminders of leadmining from a bygone age. Starting at Pateley Bridge, the route climbs over to the narrow valley of Ashfold Side, and on to the old Prosperous and Providence mines. It then crosses to the mining area of Brandstone Beck and climbs to Greenhow, the highest village in Yorkshire. Coldstones is Nidderdale's secret big hole, and the return to Pateley is through fields, farms and Fishpond Wood. There is parking off High Street and a free car park near the river.

Pateley Bridge has long been the hub of upper Nidderdale. It owes some of its early prosperity to the leadmines of Greenhow and Merryfield, particularly from about 1700 to 1850 when a large number of men from Bewerley, Pateley, and surrounding farms and cottages were employed in the mines. Pateley had a sheet-lead works near the bridge, and a lead-pipe and sheet-lead mill 'a little above the town'. In the 1750s came two new turnpike roads and, in its heyday, Pateley High Street was a closely-packed series of inns, ale-houses, hostels and shops. What was once the George still has the date of 1664, and another was called the Cat in the Window. The Miners Arms and Old Clock House were near the bridge, while the Crown is still going strong. At the top of the street, Metcalfes built the brewery in 1775 that kept all the inns stocked with the famous Pateley Ales.

From the bridge, start along the Greenhow road and, just before the first shop, turn to the right. The snicket leads up to the old Methodist chapel and brewery, now both converted to flats. Opposite the former chapel, the path climbs steeply uphill, and there are soon fine views back to the town below and the wider aspect of Nidderdale.

Pass Eagle Hall on the left, which takes its name from the family crest of the

Whites, who lived here for 150 years and owned nearby leadmines. In 1893 a convalescent home was added by Lord Mountgarret, and today the buildings are private dwellings. The two lakes are fed by water draining from Eagle Level, which was started in 1825 and driven for over a mile under Greenhow Hill, in the hope of discovering a rich vein of lead ore. Digging went on until 1844, when it was abandoned, though the tunnel helped drain water from Sunside and Cockhill mines. In 1775, near the entrance to Eagle Hall, there was a lead-smelting mill, of which there is no longer any trace.

Continue to the tarred lane and, two fields on, turn right through a wooden gate, passing down one field and left along a wall. The foxgloves here reach six feet (1.8m) in the summer, and overhead a kestrel keeps an eye open for movement in the grass.

Join a green lane to Mosscarr Bottom, where there is a footbridge over the beck and a cottage dated 1840. Cross Ashfold Side Beck at the caravan site and walk up the track on the far side of the beck. On the right is a steep flowery bank, with bluebell, pignut, rockrose and bugle, followed later in the summer by harebell, betony, wood sage and devilsbit scabious. The redstart likes this sort of habitat with scattered

The High Street, Pately Bridge; and (inset) a detail of one of its archways.

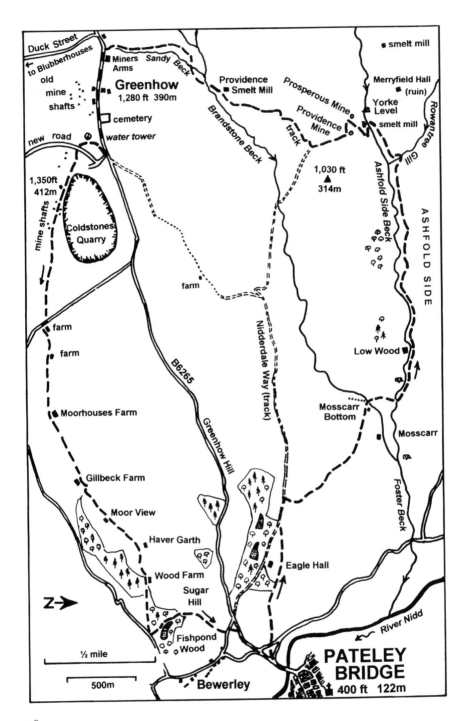

Pateley Bridge as seen from the south side of the River Nidd.

trees, and you may hear its *weet* call or catch sight of the chestnut-red tail.

The attractive wooded ravine soon becomes wooded only on one side, and then is joined by the tributary stream of Rowantree Gill coming in from the right. Growing in a streamlet near the gate are the yellow flowers of musk. A relative of the bigger monkey flower, it has smaller, unspotted yellow flowers and is very much a Nidderdale plant, being rare or absent in the other dales. The bare gravel heaps down near the beck, and mounds in the distance, are the remains of leadmining. Few plants will colonise these tips because of the poisonous metal, even after 100 years or more. Spring sandwort is one that can tolerate lead. This starry little white flower is therefore also known as leadwort.

At the finger post, descend to the beck,

the crossing of which can be difficult after heavy rain, and enter a scene of industrial archaeology. Near the beck are the remains of Prosperous dressing mill, smelt mill and shaft — the mine still has a large cog-wheel jutting out of the top of it, and a collapsed flue runs up the hill slope. Forty yards (35m) up the beck is the Yorke Level entrance, which was dug in the 1770s to drain the Merryfield mines higher up. You can see Merryfield smelt mill and chimney further up the valley.

As you wind up the hillside through the tips on the far side of the beck, you pass the site of a grinding mill, and the shafts of Prosperous and Providence mines. These mines were the most productive of all those in the Greenhow area, where the rich Merryfield vein divided into three further veins. They have been worked for hundreds

The remains of Prosperous Mine and its still-extensive waste heaps. In the leadmining process, 'dressing' the ore separated the galena from the worthless rock. This took place near the mine entrance, and a lot of finely-broken debris can still be seen at Prosperous Mine.

of years, and in the 1820s there were three large water-wheels here, one of which operated the dressing mill and the other two drove pumps for lifting water from the 200 foot (60m) deep mines.

When first brought out of the mine, the silvery ore of lead sulphide was all mixed in with rock and worthless spar — white minerals of barite and calcite, known as 'gangue'. The dressing process is the separation of the ore from the gangue and involves crushing, either by hand, when it was carried out by girls and boys using a flat hammer, or by a large hammer powered by a water wheel. Large pieces of ore were picked out by hand, and the smaller crushed material was placed in fine hand-sieves and shaken in a stream of water, where the lead sank and the lighter

material came to the top. The shaking of the sieves was mainly carried out by women. The dressed ore then went to the smelt mill to be roasted, the sulphur being driven off as a vapour.

Here, Prosperous smelt mill is conveniently placed just below the dressing mill. The remains of the flues can be traced up the hillside. They provided a good draught for the furnace and carried away the noxious fumes. But the thick, poisonous smoke must have drifted everywhere, probably killing off the surrounding vegetation. Along with the dampness and dust underground, the fumes added another threat to the miners' health.

In the 1830s there was a depression in the industry due to cheap imports, when the price of lead went down by a third and wages were halved. There was an upsurge in the late 1840s and, although mining continued until the 1880s, it was a constant struggle to keep the mines going as the ore gradually became exhausted. Among the coarser material on the tip heaps, you will find the minerals barite (creamy-white and heavy), calcite (whiter and lighter in weight), galena (lead sulphide, the silvery ore of lead), and small amounts of zinc blende (dark brown).

Above the tips, pass a lone sycamore and make for the gap in the wall ahead; then 100 yards (90m) further on, turn right into a walled lane. The track curves round and, with a left turn, makes its way into the next valley of Brandstone Beck. Much of the path is surfaced with waste from the lead-mines. On the right, two strong stone arches are all that remains of the Providence smelt mill. Cross the beck, and on the tips look for fluorite (clear with cubic crystals) in addition to barite and galena. Near a flat-roofed building the track passes over the sturdy entrance to the Gillfield Level, which drained Sunside mines round Greenhow village. According to J M Dickinson in *The Greenhow Leadmining Field*, the level appears to have been started in pre-gunpowder days, showing pick-marks rather than drill holes, and completed in 1789.

Just past the tunnel entrance, strike up to the left over a wooden stile to follow the small side-gill of Sandy Beck, due south and steeply up to Greenhow village. Pass two old mineshafts where, in May, green hairstreak butterflies flit about, the cater-pillars of which feed on bilberry.

The path emerges on the Pateley Bridge to Grassington road at the appropriately-named and strategically-placed Miners Arms, which contains several relics of lead-mining days. Mining was carried on here in Roman times, and probably before. At first the ore was dug along shallow cuts

where the veins outcropped at the surface. From the twelfth century, land in the area was granted from the Mowbray family to Fountains and Byland abbeys and, from about 1446, monks took ore from Green-how to a new smelt mill at Smelthouses. But it wasn't until the seventeenth century that houses were allowed to be built here at Greenhow Hill. In 1822 the place was well-described in *A Topographical Dictionary of Yorkshire*:

'A large straggling village, upon an eminence west of Pateley Bridge, abounding with Lead Mines and in which there are rarely less than five hundred inhabitants in this village employed. The mines are Sunside, Prosperous, Providence, Cock-hill and Merryfield which produce annually 2,000 tons.'

The church was built in 1857 in a medieval style and, at 1,280 feet (390m) above sea level, is thought to be the second highest in England — the village itself being the highest in Yorkshire. Rudyard Kipling recognised the people of this wild hill-top 'by the red-apple colour o' their cheeks an' nose tips, and their blue eyes, driven into pin-points by the wind'.

From the Miners Arms, follow the road-side footpath up through the village past the chunkiest of war memorials, made of two large blocks of Yorkshire gritstone, past the cemetery and water tower, to the entrance to Coldstones Quarry. At the quarry entrance, go through the stile in the wall on the right and pass almost underneath the same water tower.

The emergence of limestone at the sur-face — the consequence of a large anticline or upfold in the strata — not only brings lead-bearing rock within reach, but is responsible for the sweeter soils and the resulting variety of flowering plants. In spring there is a beautiful field of cowslips and, around the old leadmines, mountain pan-sies, mossy saxifrage and spring sandwort

The massive man-made limestone hole of Coldstones Quarry, the only working quarry in the dale.

brighten an exposed landscape. This area has been designated a Site of Special Scientific Interest. The surrounding moorland is the home of skylark, curlew and redshank, and you may see the short-eared owl as it flaps and turns close to the ground, hunting for small mammals.

About 100 yards (90m) past the water tower, turn left across the new quarry road and over an embankment to the rim of Coldstones Quarry. As it is on the crest of a hill, you can only see into it if you go right up to the edge. This is a very large working limestone quarry, a vast and impressive hole that descends in giant steps, and where large machines and trucks are dwarfed by its size. The quarry is worked mainly for aggregates and road metal, and from time to time old lead-workings, fresh mineral veins and natural potholes are exposed.

Walk along the rim as far as a small pond, after which gradually leave the quarry edge and follow a series of craters of old

mineshafts and bell-pits to a stile in the stone wall ahead, and aim for a cottage on the road. Turn right on to the road, then left through a farmyard. Drop down through the fields to Moor House Farm, and a ladder stile a few yards below the farm. Follow the line of an old wall, and go to the left of Gill Beck Farm to join a track to Moor View, Haver Garth and Wood Farm. Enter woodland, and leave the main track for a short descent on a grassy path through the lovely broad-leaved trees of White Wood.

Just before the road, take the stile into Fishpond Wood, where the path curves round to the left alongside the peaceful lake where bulrushes grow. After an iron kissing-gate, go up to the right, over Sugar Hill and down to the bottom far corner of a field to meet the road. Turn left, then right and across to the Grassington road for a short step down into Pateley, past the cattle market and the Royal Oak.

WALK 16: GOUTHWAITE RESERVOIR AND RAMSGILL

Start:	Pateley Bridge. Grid Ref: 158 656
Distance:	9½ miles (15km)
OS Maps:	Pathfinder 630 and 652 or Landranger 99
Walking Time:	4½ hours

Here is a walk for the birdwatcher. Mostly on the level, it begins in Pateley Bridge and roughly follows the former railway line via Wath as far as Bouthwaite, along the pleasant east side of Gouthwaite Reservoir. After visiting the pretty village of Ramsgill, the walk proceeds along the road, the only choice on the west side of the reservoir, so please take care. The route then leaves the road to visit Heathfield, descends to the Watermill Inn, and makes for the river and a return to Pateley Bridge. There is car parking along Nidd Walk by the river in Pateley. Bring a good bird book and a pair of binoculars.

Pateley Bridge is the tourist centre of up-per Nidderdale and has a population of 2,500. It first began to receive visitors in any numbers after the railway line was opened on the 1st May 1862. The North Eastern Railway ran excursions from the industrial towns of Leeds, Halifax and Doncaster, describing the area rather hope-fully as 'the Switzerland of England'. A tourist guide, written soon afterwards by John Thorpe, told of 'the beauties of Netherdale and its adjacent mountain scen-ery', and talked of 'vast and beautiful treas-ures of nature laid open to public view by the introduction of railways'. People came to see How Stean Gorge, to stroll along the riverbank or, from Panorama Walk, obtain a very impressive bird's-eye view of the dale.

Constructed on the site of a former gla-cial lake, Gouthwaite Reservoir was com-pleted in 1900 and entirely transformed the scenery of the upper dale. Because of its attraction to a great number and variety of birds, in 1978 it was made a nature reserve, and has become a well-known birdwatching locality and a Site of Special Scientific In-terest.

By 1908 the Nidd Valley Light Railway, built by Bradford Corporation, was open from Pateley to Angram in preparation for building the upper reservoirs, and passen-gers could go as far as Lofthouse, with sta-tions at Wath and Ramsgill. This line was closed in 1936.

The railway to Pateley Bridge, too, is gone — closed in 1964 — but there are now even more visitors to this attractive town, with its busy village atmosphere. At Christmas, the steep High Street is graced by a wonderful array of lighted Christmas trees, replaced in summer by colourful hanging baskets and flower displays. In the shops, pubs and eating places, a cheerful welcome awaits you. There are craft work-shops with potters and glass-blowers, gal-leries and antique shops and, for a reminder of the town's past, the Nidderdale Museum in King Street has some fine displays of stone-quarrying and reservoir-building. It was set up in former council offices and part of the old workhouse and, in 1990, received the Small Museum of the Year award.

Starting from the bridge at Pateley, take the path up the right side of the river, soon coming alongside it by a fine weir and mill race. The Nidd alternates between quiet, peaceful stretches and sections where it fairly rushes along, always shrouded by trees, mainly alders. The path joins the line

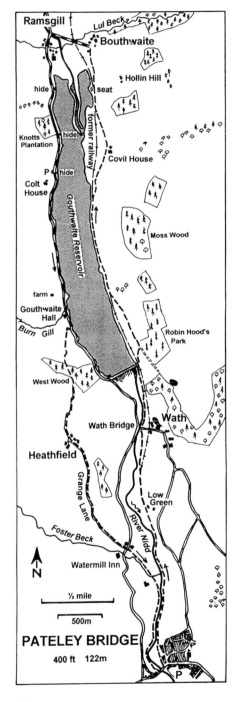

of the former railway, and, near the village of Wath, crosses a wooden plank bridge over Dauber Gill to the road.

Wath is Norse for ford, and there was probably one in use when a grange of Fountains Abbey was established here. A bridge over the Nidd was built in the twelfth century, when monks from Byland Abbey had rights to pass over Fountains' land (Fountains Earth) *en route* to their granges at Ramsgill, Gouthwaite and Heathfield. A five foot (1.5m) wide packhorse bridge had certainly stood here for some time, but was only wide enough for pedestrians and horses. The Victorian historian, Harry Speight, tells of how farmers with a cart would occasionally take a short cut and squeeze over the bridge 'by removing one wheel and pushing the axle along the parapet of the bridge!' In 1890, the bridge was enlarged to double its width — and it is still a most graceful stone arch. A few years later, a farmhouse was converted to an inn for men working on the new reservoir — it is now the Sportsmans Arms — and the railway station was built across the way.

Continue along the riverbank. Marsh marigolds, cuckoo flower and large bittercress grow in a wet patch, along with marsh thistle which can be white, pink or purple. Soon part of the dam comes into view through the trees and, when the reservoir is full, provides a picturesque water-drop, an attractive scene decorated by arches and castellated towers.

The path climbs to the top corner of the next field, to join a lane with wonderful views of the lake, the far side of the valley and downdale to Guisecliff. The lane gently descends to the lakeside and, by now, you will have been aware of some of the birds attracted to this lovely expanse of water.

In spring and early summer, pairs of common sandpiper inhabit the shore, and among the common birds are moorhen, mallard, coot and tufted duck, the last one being black with a head plume and a white side-patch. Look out for the occasional heron stalking fish in the shallows, and large numbers of Canada geese which may be grazing on the bank or forming a large flotilla on the lake. Have a good look for a stranger amongst them for, in winter, it could be a white-fronted goose.

Along the track there are plenty of bluetits, dunnocks, robins and goldfinches, enough to attract the sparrowhawk in a surprise attack. Swallows, house martins and swifts swoop and dive both over the water and the fields, while black-headed gulls seek insects in the grass or join jackdaws to find a good up-current to lift them above the steep slopes.

Pass Covil House, site of another grange of Fountains Abbey, and just when you might appreciate a rest, a seat has been provided overlooking the shallow end of the reservoir. Among the ducks, the handsome male wigeon has a blond quiff on the front of his chestnut head, and in summer you may be lucky to see a shoveler, with a huge, broad bill, the male having an orange side-patch and green head. There are usually teal present, with especially large numbers in the autumn. Pochard and goldeneye are winter visitors. Occasionally a cormorant is seen, much to the consternation of fishermen.

Continue to Bouthwaite, where the monks of Fountains had another grange. Robert Innman, known as 'Bold Robin of Bouthwaite', lived at the grange and is said to have killed several thieves with a dagger that was kept in the family. In 1648, at the

Gouthwaite, finished in 1900, was built to act as a compensation reservoir, storing plentiful water during the winter and releasing it during the drier summer to maintain an even flow in the River Nidd. It has been a nature reserve since 1978 because of the number and variety of birds which breed or visit here.

Canada geese are common on Gouthwaite Reservoir. They were introduced as an ornamental bird from North America during the seventeenth century, and the last fifty years has seen a rapid increase in numbers.

age of sixty-four, he fought on the side of Parliament when the king's men took Pateley Bridge, and narrowly escaped being made prisoner. The initials RI of Bold Robin's grandson are still to be seen over the door of the rebuilt grange, dated 1673.

At Bouthwaite, turn left along the road, crossing Lul Beck where the remains of the former railway bridge can be seen, then left over the Nidd and into the pretty village of Ramsgill. The small group of buildings looks on to an open green, the Yorke Arms dominating the scene. The church is nineteenth century, but behind it there is a gable of a chapel of Byland Abbey.

With great care and attention to traffic, continue along the road which skirts the reservoir. Fly-fishing in the lake is carried on enthusiastically for a catch of wild brown trout and grayling. The grayling go up the streams to spawn in the spring, and the trout in the autumn.

The wall along the road makes a good hide from which to see more birds over the water, but three simple hides have been created just off the road, overlooking the lake. Sometimes you see birders not just with binoculars and telescope but with radio communication too, as they wait for the rarity, a dot in the sky, perhaps, which may turn out to be a peregrine, goshawk, hen harrier or even an osprey, any of which are likely to be seen in the winter months. In 1970 a young golden eagle stayed for three months, so there is always the thrill of some exciting possibilities for those with patience and experience.

Pass Gouthwaite Bridge over the sidestream of Burn Gill, then Gouthwaite Hall with its clipped yews and stone-mullioned windows. The original hall was pulled down

before the reservoir was filled, and was the birthplace of Dr William Craven, who was taught by Eugene Aram, and who went on to become professor of Arabic and master of his college at Cambridge.

About 200 yards (180m) further on, near a bend in the road, turn off acutely to the right over a cattle grid, along a quiet byroad known as Grange Lane up to Heathfield. Up to the right, there are signs of iron-mining and smelting. Heathfield is listed in *Domesday Book*, and Roger de Mobray, the founder of Byland Abbey, gave pasture here for eighty mares and their foals. An abbey grange was established, and the farm of Colt House (halfway along the reservoir) for the horses. In early Norman times, Heathfield was the only place of any significance above Pateley Bridge, and was the centre of the township of Stonebeck Down. Heathfield is now just a few farms on the shoulder of a hill at the meeting place of several tracks and footpaths, three of which go over to the leadmining area of Ashfold Side.

Follow the lane down the hill, with fine views ahead of Pateley Bridge, the dale down to Guisecliff and beyond. The roadside is bordered by foxgloves, herb robert, cow parsley and germander speedwell. At Fosterbeck road junction, go through the stile on the left to join the built-up bank of the murmuring stream of Foster Beck itself, bordered with willows and alders. Fosterbeck flax mill, which specialised in string-making, is now the Watermill Inn, and still retains its fine thirty-four foot (10m) waterwheel, restored in 1990. Leave Foster Beck and cross a field to reach the banks of the River Nidd and a return to Pateley Bridge.

WALK 17: MOORLAND WALK FROM RAMSGILL TO LOFTHOUSE

Start: *Ramsgill. Grid Ref: 119 710*
Distance: *9 miles (14 km)*
OS Maps: *Pathfinder 630 or Landranger 99*
Walking Time: *4 hours*

Here is a walk for those who like to stride out on open moorland, where the senses may be sharpened by the sound of the curlew in spring or the delicate perfume of heather in summer. Starting in the lovely village of Ramsgill, it climbs to Fountains Earth Moor along an ancient track to 1,300 feet (400m) above sea level, with a view of the curiously-named rocks Jenny Twigg and her Daughter Tib. A short descent of Trapping Hill brings you into Lofthouse, with a return through the fields to Ramsgill. The village of Ramsgill lies above Pateley Bridge at the top end of Gouthwaite Reservoir, and there is limited parking by the village green.

Ramsgill — the name is of Norse origin — is one of the most attractive villages in Nidderdale. Nineteenth-century stone cottages, village hall, circular pound and the Yorke Arms, complete with virginia creeper, cluster in picturesque fashion round the green. A fine horse chestnut tree dominates the green, and not far along is the copper beech planted in 1897 to commemorate Queen Victoria's jubilee.

The village is sited where two tributary streams join the Nidd and, in monastic

The Yorke Arms, the fountain and the horse trough on Ramsgill village green.

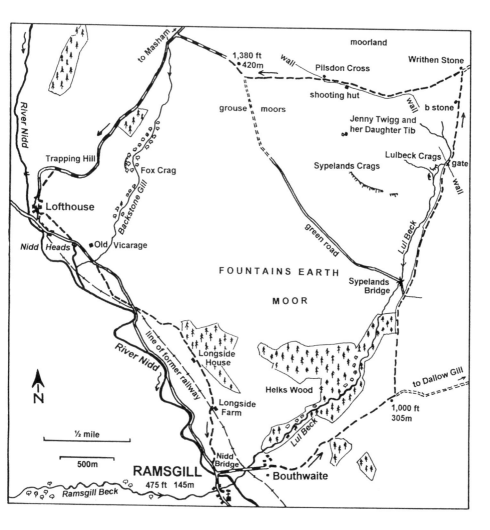

times, routes reached Ramsgill grange, not just from up and down the dale, but also from Kirkby Malzeard over Fountains Earth Moor. In 1546 after the Dissolution, surrounding lands — the 'forests of Heathfield and Middlesmoor' — were purchased for the sum of £800 by John Yorke of London, and estates remained in the family for nearly 400 years until 1924. In their early years, the Yorkes lived at nearby Gouthwaite Hall (now beneath the reservoir), and later they moved down the dale to Bewerley Old Hall.

In 1704 the notorious Eugene Aram was born in Ramsgill. A brilliant scholar in Greek, Latin, Hebrew, Celtic and mathematics, Aram set up a school in Knaresborough lower down the dale. In 1745, while he was a schoolmaster there, the shoemaker Daniel Clarke disappeared with valuable goods and, soon after, Aram also left town. Some thirteen years later, a

The little purple flowers of ivy-leaved toadflax are found on laneside walls.

former acquaintance of Aram proclaimed that the remains of Daniel Clarke would be found in St Robert's Cave by the river in Knaresborough. The skeleton was discovered, and Aram was arrested in Kings Lynn while teaching at the grammar school there. He was imprisoned in York, and at his trial 'delivered a defence so admirable for its ingenuity, and so replete with erudition and antiquarian knowledge, that it astonished the whole court'. However, he was convicted for the murder and was hung at York in 1759, after which his body was displayed on the Knaresborough gibbet.

In a short history of Ramsgill and its church, local historian Eileen Crabtree gives a more complete story of Eugene Aram, and adds other tales of village personalities and notes of interesting buildings.

Start the walk along the road up the dale over Nidd Bridge — the monks used a bridge here that was mentioned in an 1184 charter of Fountains Abbey. Turn right on the little road to Bouthwaite, where a mature Spanish chestnut stands in the woodland near the corner. Along the roadside grow leopard's bane, a tall, bright yellow, daisy-like flower, and wood cranesbill, a geranium with large pinkish-purple flowers. Pass the Wesleyan chapel to go straight on up the track to the moors. Whereas Ramsgill had a grange of Byland Abbey, Bouthwaite grange belonged to Fountains, for we have now passed into the parish of Fountains Earth.

Swallows and house martins have learned to live with man to their mutual benefit. These graceful birds find convenient nest sites around the eves of buildings, and in return rid the farmer or householder of a considerable number of insects. On the track up the hill, I watched a green woodpecker search for ants, larvae or berries in the bank. The red crown, black face and yellow-green rump made for a spectacular close-up view as it hopped along.

The track climbs along the right side of Lul Beck to open moor. It was down this ancient route that, in September 1323, King Edward II and his retinue came on their way from Kirkby Malzeard to Bewerley, calling at Ramsgill grange on their way. This track was improved only in 1811 as a route through from Masham, across Nidderdale to the rich leadmines of Grassington.

A group of large, angular rocks with an overhang, known as Sypelands Crags, come into view. Keep right where a lane branches off to the left (a possible short cut and right of way). The next rocky outcrop is Lulbeck Crags, left upstanding at the confluence of two small becks. Fountains Earth Moor consists of a fair amount of heather, with resident grouse, moorland grasses and rushes. In early summer, the trackside is decorated with the small, pale blue flowers of heath speedwell, white tufts of heath bedstraw and the tiny, rather insignificant white flowers of spring whitlow grass.

On the open moor there are curlews in all directions, meadow pipits galore and the whinchat. This attractive little summer visitor has a white eye-stripe and white patches at the side of the tail. The whinchat will find a prominent perch, where it flicks its wings and tail. A close view shows its lovely peachy-coloured breast. You might also catch sight of a buzzard making circles in the sky, or hear the plaintive call of the golden plover — a liquid whistle of *klew-ee*.

The next wall (with gate) is the final one, the intake wall and the last of the enclosures; built in 1855, the wall runs as straight as a die across the moor. At the junction of tracks is the Writhen Stone, marked with a broad arrow benchmark to indicate 1,350 feet (411m) above sea level. The Masham track goes off to the right, but turn left here in an easterly direction for nearly two miles (3km) to the Lofthouse/Masham road.

The open moorland road passes through broad expanses of heather moor, then joins the intake wall. From near the shooting hut you can obtain a good view of the upright rocks, the figures of Jenny Twigg and her Daughter Tib, the origin of the names being lost in time. At the gate, Pilsdon Cross, mentioned in a charter of 1259, is somewhat hidden by the gatepost. There is still heather in every direction. On fine days in late October and early November, after shooting has finished, long strips of old heather are 'swiddened' or burned to encourage new young shoots, and plumes of smoke are a common sight.

Where the route rejoins the lane from Sypelands, the walk reaches its highest point, 1,380 feet (420m) above sea level on the slopes of High Ash Head Moor. In the flat-topped Pennine landscape, Great Whernside hardly stands out, though to the left the more conical-shaped hump of Meugher breaks the monotonous skyline.

At the Lofthouse/Masham road, turn down the steep section known as Trapping Hill, with views down the dale to Gouthwaite and Backstone Gill on the left. Cut off the last bend in the road where it enters an unfenced section, to follow a line of trees directly down to the village of Lofthouse. The name, meaning 'a house with a loft or second floor', is Norse and was sometimes used in the plural. This attractive cluster of stone-built houses, with pub and shop-cum-post office, has a long history. An important grange and dairy farm built here belonged to Fountains Abbey, and the Raynor family, keepers of the grange, supplied substantial quantities of butter and cheese to the monks. Farming has been the main concern ever since, moving to beef-rearing and sheep. Lofthouse marks the head of the valley, and was the passenger terminus for the Nidd Valley Light Railway from Pateley Bridge.

Opposite the door of the village institute, a stile takes you across a field or two to the road at Nidd Heads. It is here that the underground Nidd re-emerges in powerful springs. Turning left, keep to the road for 330 yards (300m), crossing Backstone Beck and passing the Old Vicarage, to find a stile on the right. After a couple of fields, cross the road where the railway used to cross it, but after another 100 yards (90m) along the line of the railway, climb steeply to the lower edge of a larch plantation, from where there are good views of the dale. Pass behind the beautifully-positioned Longside House, a youth hostel until 1983 and, on a gentle descent, cross a farm track to continue down the grassy slope to Longside Farm. Pass below the farm and through river meadows to the road and a return to Ramsgill.

WALK 18: HOW STEAN GORGE

Start: *How Stean Gorge car park. Grid Ref: 098 733*
Distance: *4 miles (6½km)*
OS Maps: *Outdoor Leisure Map 30 or Landranger 99*
Walking Time: *2½ hours*

This walk has a wide variety of scenery over a short distance. First a visit to the famous gorge itself, for which there is a charge (open all year). The gorge is for those who are sure-footed and have a good head for heights, and a good torch is needed to go through the cave. The walk then explores the higher part of the valley as far as High Riggs, from where there is a steep descent to cross the beck via large boulders, and returns through the hamlet of Stean. If you are travelling up the dale, Lofthouse is eight miles (13km) beyond Pateley Bridge. Keep left at the junction at Lofthouse, then left again for the How Stean private car/coach park, on the left before the bridge.

The limestone gorge of How Stean is one of the tourist attractions of Nidderdale, and this showpiece of miniature scenery is all the more striking because of the contrast with the sombre surroundings of the gritstone moorland. It is a surprising place, and best seen and appreciated by going down into the gorge itself. The valley of How Stean is a major tributary of the Nidd and here, where the two valleys come together near Lofthouse, a patch of pure limestone appears at the surface like an island surrounded by millstone grit. Geologists refer to it as a window — looking through a hole, as it were, worn in the millstone grit cover.

Beginning the walk at the car park, pause at the bridge over the beck to see how the stream has cut deep into the limestone, leaving it scalloped and hollowed-out by the action of water. The narrow, sheltered gorge is well-wooded, and in the early summer has a good variety of wild flowers. Tickets are obtained at the cottage, where you can get a booklet with a detailed map of the gorge and caves, or hire a torch to explore the cave.

Having entered the gorge, it is not long before vertical walls of limestone and overhangs face the visitor. From the first

footbridge you can see wild brown trout in the waters below, and the rocks nearby display the fossil stems of crinoids — looking like segmented worms. Just up from the bridge is Tom Taylor's Cave, and all you need is a torch to walk through one of the safest of cave passages. There are no obstacles, and if you go to the end (180 yards/160m) you emerge near the café car park in a ring wall known as Cat Hole. In 1868, two boys found thirty-two Roman coins on a ledge in the cave. They are now displayed in the museum in York.

The narrow path alongside the gorge crosses the second footbridge over a fifty foot (15m) ravine, and then the visitor has to walk, with head bent to avoid an overhang, along a narrow shelf of rock on the very rim of the gorge. At the far end of the path is a wider platform of rock and an ivy-hung cliff, the site of a former quarry. To the left, How Stean Tunnel brings a small side-beck under the road, while upstream the gorge narrows abruptly where it winds between vertical rock-walls above dark, deep water. The limestone underfoot here is crowded with fossil crinoid stems.

In early summer there is a wealth of wild flowers and ferns in the gorge, typical of a site on limestone. Herb robert, wild garlic and dog's mercury are common, but among them you may find large bittercress, wood sanicle and sweet woodruff. The bittercress is rather like a large white cuckoo flower, in which the young blooms have purple-headed stamens. Wood sanicle is of the parsley family and has white pom-pom flowers. Sweet woodruff, one of the bedstraws, has white flowers with a lovely delicate fragrance. The ferns include harts-tongue, maidenhair spleenwort and brittle bladder fern.

If you have an ear for birdsong you will pick out, even above the rushing sound of the beck, the loud voice of the wren, the chirpy song of the robin and the clear sound of the song thrush. The spotted flycatcher may show itself by settling momentarily on an obvious perch, before dashing for another insect and returning to the same spot.

Exit the gorge either by going through Tom Taylor's Cave or by the higher path that comes out at the café. Continue up the lane, towards the hamlet of Stean, but before you get there, go through the stone stile on the right (by a caravan), where, in summer, melancholy thistle and wood cranes-bill grow among young saplings. Cross the footbridge, with another view deep into the limestone gorge, and, rather than take the Nidderdale Way, turn left through a series of stiles and flowery meadows with the beck on the left. Pass a limekiln, lined with gritstone, reddened by the heat of the working kiln. There is a lovely dell here where, in late spring, there is the scent of May blossom and the orange-tip butterfly patrols the stream bank. By autumn, the berries attract fieldfares and redwings.

Step up to the right, to continue along a wooded section with a wide variety of trees, and pass beneath the trunk of a fallen larch supported on one or two of its slender limbs. There are open glades full of wild flowers and the songs of the blackcap, robin and willow warbler. Among the ferns are

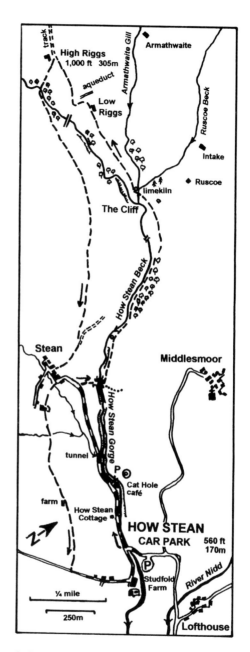

lady fern, with large, delicate, feathery fronds, and male fern. The latter has large circular sori or spore sacs, five or six on the back of each leaflet. The more numerous and narrow sori on lady fern are often comma-shaped and the leaflets are further divided. Flowers include meadow saxifrage and yellow pimpernel, and you may catch sight of roe deer in this area, too.

The path climbs to a high point, and a branch leads off to the right to Middlesmoor. Keep on up the valley, descending to where it opens out to cross a stone bridge over the side beck of Armathwaite Gill. The small limekiln by the bridge is decorated with polypody fern and blue germander speedwell, while the beck displays a sequence of limestone, shale and sandstone, a place known locally as the Cliff.

Leave the beauties of the wooded gorge, and make your way up through field pastures to Low Riggs Farm. A good farm track leads up to High Riggs, 1,000 feet (305m) above sea level. After passing through a gate, turn off the track in front of the derelict farmhouse, which has a wonderful view down the valley of How Stean. All ramblers passing this way dream of how they might convert the old buildings into an idyllic retreat.

The path follows the left side of a small spring-fed stream, and leads down into the upper part of the wooded gorge of Stean Beck. There is an easier zigzag, or a more direct descent that can be an unpleasant, steep scramble. Cross the beck at the foot of the slope via large boulders to a wire fence, where a rock acts as a stile, and climb diagonally up the far bank. You have now crossed from Stonebeck Up to Stonebeck Down, as the beck forms the parish boundary, not just here, but for all of its 6 mile (10km) length from the slopes of Meugher

The derelict farmhouse of High Riggs, at the head of the valley of How Stean Beck.

Cottages at Stean village, a peaceful and attractive little hamlet.

to the beck's confluence with the Nidd. The small villages of Middlesmoor and Ramsgill are the centres of the two parishes which both include wild areas of the upper dale.

The path from here to Stean is pleasant enough, along the sloping hillside of the dale, though not always easy to follow. As you come up out of the gorge, you go over a rise to a metal gate with a stile on the right. Go to the right of the barn ahead, to a small stile in the wall, and aim to the right of the next two barns. Cross a small side-valley, and soon join the farm track that leads to Stean.

Stean is an attractive group of cottages, where plum trees grow in the gardens and in wild corners. Turn down the hill and, opposite the last cottage, take the stile on the right to a small wooden footbridge and the field path to Hub Hill. There are excellent views across to Middlesmoor on the hill over the How Stean valley, and ahead into Nidderdale. Follow the stone wall all the way, with good stiles. After crossing a side stream, enter the farmyard of Whitbeck Farm. Turn left then immediately right, round the lower side of the buildings, still following the wall along the contour. Join the lane, known as Hub Hill, and descend steeply past some interesting old farmhouses to the bottom of the hill, turning left past Studfold Farm caravan site, to return to the bridge over the beck and the start of the walk.

WALK 19: GOYDEN POT AND DALE EDGE

Start: *Lofthouse. Grid Ref: 102 734*
Distance: *10 miles (16km)*
OS Maps: *Outdoor Leisure Map 30 or Landranger 99*
Walking Time: *5 hours*

This fine, exhilarating walk includes the curved glacial trough of upper Nidderdale, first explored from below with glimpses of the appearing and disappearing Nidd, then, after a climb of 650 feet (200m), seen from above — from along Dale Edge — with magnificent views over the length of the upper dale to the reservoirs and beyond. Lofthouse is eight miles (13km) higher up the dale from Pateley Bridge, and there is a small car park in the village.

Lofthouse is a neat village, where the road winds between old farmhouses and picturesque cottages raised up on the hill slopes above the Nidd, and where, among the cluster of stone buildings, there is a friendly post office/shop, a hotel and village hall.

In an old directory the name is Lofthouses or Loftus, from the Norse meaning 'house or houses with a loft or second floor'.

The village is the only one in the township of Fountains Earth, where the monks had a large grange and dairy farm which

The war memorial fountain and village shop at the centre of Lofthouse.

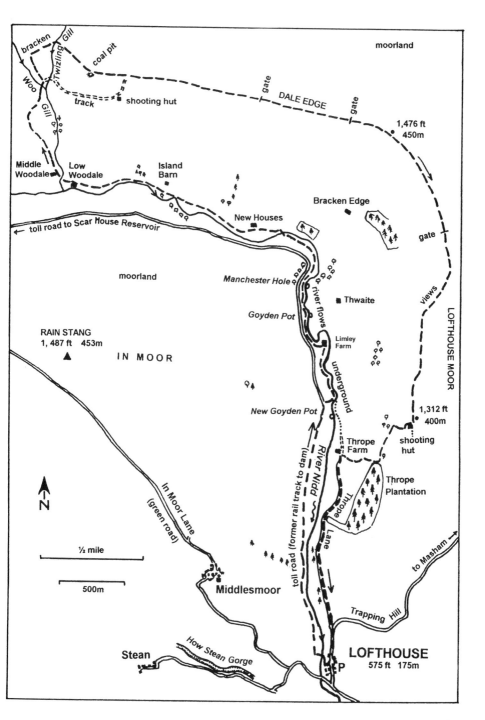

supplied butter and cheese to Fountains Abbey. Across the river, the land belonged to Byland Abbey. In the twentieth century, for nearly thirty years, until 1936, Lofthouse became the passenger terminus of the Nidd Valley Light Railway, built by Bradford Corporation to facilitate the building of the two dams at the dale head.

The village is still the main centre for the upper dale, though, until the 1960s, the only way out was by footpath or moorland track for walkers only. There are short roads that lead on to Stean, Middlesmoor and to Scar House Reservoir, but a narrow road now climbs through Lofthouse village, steeply up over the moors to Colsterdale and Masham.

Starting the walk from the fountain memorial at the centre of the village, go to the left of Fountain Cottage along a path to the stone packhorse bridge over the Nidd, where limestone outcrops in the river bed. Cross the bridge and walk up the reservoir toll road, formerly the track of the railway. Not far along you may hear the sound of Nidd Falls and, on a fine day in early summer, with a cuckoo calling in the background and blackcap singing in the wood, in the more open parts you might see the yellow wagtail, a slim, graceful bird with bright yellow underparts and greenish back, or its cousins, the pied and grey wagtails. The green woodpecker can also be seen here, dull green with a red crown, and rather timid. In flight it swoops along, closing its wings every three or four beats, yellow rump in evidence.

Along the roadside grow wild roses, wood cranesbill, herb bennet and common spotted orchid. Wood cranesbill is a lovely native geranium, with pinkish-purple flowers and white centre, contrasting with the smaller, yellow flowers of herb bennet (or wood avens).

Keep to the road for just over a mile (1.9km). Pass the track to Thrope Farm and then a line of pine trees on the right. A few paces further there is a stile, which takes you down to the riverbank. The woodland path passes the neat entrance to an old coalmine, an adit or horizontal tunnel in the riverbank. At Limley Farm, go immediately left of the farmhouse to continue along the left side of the more-or-less dry riverbed. Sandstone is seen here and there at the surface, for the underlying limestone is completely hidden along this stretch.

At Goyden Pot, the white limestone appears again as a small cliff, capped with trees, with large boulders in front of the gaping cave entrance at its foot. The boulders contain the fossil shells of *Gigantoproductus* as white, calcite, crescent-shaped cross-sections. The riverbed above the cave is of clean stones and boulders and, though usually dry, will carry surplus water when the river is high. Tony Waltham gives a warning if the river is in flood:

'It is an awesome sight when the river does flow into Goyden Pot; the water sluices down the entrance passage at great speed. On no account should it be entered . . . '

When the riverbed is completely dry, it is safe to do a little exploring. With a good torch it is possible to enter the first passage, ten feet (3m) high and wide, as far as a triple junction; beyond this it is most advisable to have proper caving equipment and knowledge of the passages, as described in Tony Waltham's *Yorkshire Dales: Limestone Country*. The riverbed below Goyden Pot is higher than the cave entrance and covered with grass, indicating that it is very unusual for floodwater to overflow into this section.

Continue along the left side of the river and, opposite a stile from the road, cross the riverbed for a peep at the real Nidd as it rushes on its subterranean way in Manchester Hole. At low water, with care you can scramble down into the hole to see the

A panoramic view of upper Nidderdale from Dale Edge: Great Whernside, Little Whernside and Dead Man's Hill, and Scar House Reservoir.

flow of the river and experience the rushing sound that is magnified to a roar.

Proceed along the tree-lined river, which soon reappears to flow on the surface, cross the wooden footbridge (before reaching a barn) and on to New Houses. Fountains Abbey once had a dairy farm here, but none of the original buildings exist. Go past the front of the farmhouse and to the river bridge. The path carries on along the right side of the river on a broad track. Views of the steep Dale Edge up to the right and of the return route emphasise the broad curve in the valley at this point, steepened by the ice as, some 20,000 years ago, it swung in its slow, grinding way to the south. Still keeping near to the river, there are some well-built stone stiles, and Low Woodale is the next objective.

Along this stretch, there's another chance of seeing the grey and pied wagtails. The grey likes to be near the river, perching on rocks or overhanging trees, and often nests on the bank. Although yellow beneath, its back is grey and the wagging tail is obviously longer than that of the pied wagtail. A wet patch just before the farm has marsh marigold, and later ragged robin and marsh stitchwort, while hawkweed, monkey flower and forget-me-not grow on the bank behind.

Go through the farmyard of Low Woodale — the old farmhouse is on the far left with stone-mullioned windows — and straight on, on a track that takes you to Middle Woodale. On the way, pause for a dramatic view of Scar House Dam. A rookery in the trees at Middle Woodale was noted by the writer Harry Speight almost 100 years ago, and it is still there today. The Woodale farms lie in the most tranquil part of the dale, and represent a long period of rural history when, along with many other families, generations of Horners lived here. Simon, one of their descendants, founded the school in Middlesmoor in 1803.

Climbing out of the valley at Middle Woodale, strike uphill to the left of a wooded ravine, continuing up the hillside by a broken wall to a gate and wide track through the bracken.

Descend to Woo Gill and, eighty yards (75m) after crossing the bridge, turn up to the left through the bracken, turning right as the slope flattens out. After crossing Twizling Gill, the track follows the contour to a large abandoned coalmine, where, on the tip, there are fossil roots of coal-measure trees. The fossil is named *Stigmaria* — usually seen as symmetrical rows of dots — and represents the roots of more than one species of tree.

The high-level walk along Dale Edge, for nearly three miles (5km) along a good track, is among patchy heather and tussocky grass, where red grouse, golden plover, curlew and meadow pipit all stake out their territories. The plump grouse may erupt suddenly from the ground in a flurry of wings, telling you to 'go-back, go-back', while the meadow pipit sings its twittery song overhead, before gliding earthwards — wings down and tail up. Both the golden plover and curlew have far-reaching, yet melancholy calls, sounds so much a part of the heather moorland scene that they can send a chill down the spine of a sensitive listener.

On a clear day, views of the dale are very extensive. In the distance Great and Little Whernside have flat outlines, and below them the two reservoirs occupy the top end of the valley, while further over to the left, Meugher's slight cone-shape protrudes above the level skyline.

Just before the stone shooting hut with tower, dated 1912, the path begins its steep descent to a gate. Nearby lie four stone gateposts, apparently unused; presumably they were quarried nearby. The path descends through scattered birch and bracken, and down the edge of a mature conifer plantation to Thrope Farm. Turn left along Thrope Lane, a sunken grassy track. Pass above another plantation, first conifer then broad-leaved, to get a view across to Middlesmoor on the hilltop before a gentle descent into Lofthouse.

WALK 20: MIDDLESMOOR AND SCAR HOUSE RESERVOIR

Start: *Middlesmoor. Grid Ref: 092 742*
Distance: *8½ miles (13½km)*
OS Maps: *Outdoor Leisure Map 30 or Landranger 99*
Walking Time: *4½ hours*

Starting from the picturesquely-situated village of Middlesmoor, this walk first descends into the upper dale, then crosses onto a mid-level track known as the Edge, here following the Nidderdale Way. It climbs to Woo Gill, after which there are fine views of the two reservoirs, and Great and Little Whernside. The route crosses the impressive Scar House Dam and returns along the high-level lane over Rain Stang. Middlesmoor lies on a hilltop, one mile (1.6km) beyond Lofthouse, and there is a small car park at the upper end of the village.

Facing south and with breathtaking views on three sides, Middlesmoor stands 940 feet (285m) above sea level on the shoulder of the hill between the valleys of the upper Nidd and that of How Stean. At the dale head, its isolation, dominant position and appealing cluster of stone buildings, crowned by the church tower, make it the most attractive of villages.

Before the church was licensed in 1484, christenings, weddings and burials were performed in Kirkby Malzeard, twelve miles away over the moors to the east, a hazardous journey along the old corpse road.

The present church was completely re-built in 1865 and contains an ancient stone known as St Chad's Cross, named after the seventh century Celtic bishop of Ripon. The elevated site of the church may well have been that of a pre-Christian shrine, consecrated by St Chad for Christian use. The church has a peal of bells, and in June a bell festival takes place to celebrate their installation. An old poster reads:

'Bell-ringing festival at Middlesmoor. Sports, refreshments and Grand Dance in the evening.'

A custom at weddings here is for local children to fasten the church gates with string during the wedding service, only allowing the bride and groom to pass through after they have thrown them silver coins.

Start the walk by going to the left of the church, between the cottages, then down across two fields, a strip of conifer woodland and a series of stone stiles, to cross the reservoir toll-road and end up on the riverbank of the Nidd. Many of the field stiles are of fine construction, each with steps leading up to two stout uprights built into the wall, making a handsome squeeze-through type. The fields have a variety of flowers, including yellow rattle, indicating an ancient meadow; and wet patches have marsh marigold, musk, ragged robin and cuckoo flower.

Cross the river at the stone bridge with an iron rail and, in front of Thrope Farm, turn left along the lane. From the bridge you may see grey wagtail, swallows and house martins around the farm and, perched prominently on a branch by the footpath, look out for the spotted flycatcher as it makes a dash for an insect. Along Thrope Lane, the route is signed 'Nidderdale Way', which this walk follows all the way back to Middlesmoor. Where the path approaches the dry riverbed (by some dead trees), at the foot of the opposite bank there is a narrow opening in the limestone. This is New Goyden Pot, where underground

Middlesmoor from Hard Gap Lane. At nearly a thousand feet above sea level, this isolated village at the head of Nidderdale stands in a commanding position on the shoulder of Rain Stang, giving panoramic views both up and down the dale.

passages extend upstream through Goyden Pot to Manchester Hole. The *Northern Caves* guide describes it as 'a major river cave with a superb railway-tunnel main streamway'.

Cross the riverbed, and pass the coal-mine tip and mine entrance to arrive at Limley Farm. Here, go between the farm buildings to the rear, and cross the river-bed again.

Just opposite is a high cliff with ash trees, where jackdaws nest and the goldfinch sings its twittering song. In summer, listen for the *weet* of the redstart. The path zigzags back up the wooded hillside, where a wych elm has beautifully arched branches.

The view from Middlesmoor churchyard, with Gouthwaite Reservoir in the middle distance.

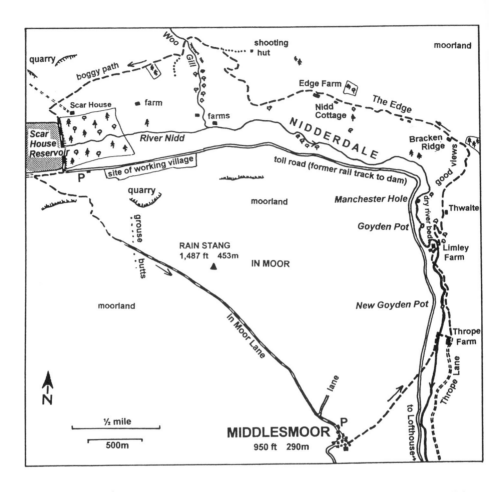

At Thwaite House — both Thrope and Thwaite were originally granges of Fountains Abbey — there still exists an ice house, a sort of old-fashioned fridge and now a listed building. Walkers are welcome at Thwaite, where teas and home cooking are available at weekends, and there is a 'rambler's relief' to the rear.

Continue along the track known as the Edge, as distinct from Dale Edge higher up *(traversed in walk 19)*, and pause to admire the panoramic views up and down the dale. The track makes exceptional walking, and links a series of farms that have fine sites

on the valley side, face the sun and have unrivalled views.

Where the path turns more sharply to the left, there are new views up the dale to Scar House Dam and Little Whernside. Nearby, a small stream descending from the pine woods has on its banks marsh thistle, visited by green-veined white butterflies; lots of heath bedstraw and bog stitchwort, both white; and yellow pimpernel, a creeper with a star of five petals, and tormentil, also yellow but more square with four petals. Continue above Bracken Ridge and Summerstone Lodge to Nidd Cottage, Edge Farm

Approaching the River Nidd from Middlesmoor, with Thrope Farm on the other side of the river. Above is Lofthouse Moor, with the two high-level routes of the Edge, traversed in this walk, and Dale Edge (see walk 19), marked by the shooting hut on the moortop.

and New Houses Edge, after which there is a gentle descent. Still on a good track, turn up fairly steeply, eventually to follow white-topped posts along the hillside to join a shooting track — a climb of 400 feet (120m) along this section.

Descend into the sheltered hollow of Woo Gill, a stream that comes down from Woogill Tarn on the side of Great Haw, a breeding site for the black-headed gull. In this area I have often noticed the green tiger beetle (bright green with pale spots, about ¾ inch or 2cm long) sunning itself on the path. This fierce carnivore — of no danger to the walker! — is a fast-running beetle and, when disturbed, takes off on a short, noisy flight. Cross the plank bridge and then, on reaching the wall at the top of the sloping track, turn up to the right to

contour along a green path above Firth Plantation.

From here there are extensive views of the two reservoirs of Scar House and Angram, and beyond to Great and Little Whernside which lie 2,310 and 1,984 feet (704m and 604m) above sea level. There is a marshy section where you may have to pick your way. Then, crossing the track to the quarry, you arrive at the massive Scar House Dam.

The reservoir forms part of Bradford's large waterworks scheme, which includes Angram higher up and Gouthwaite below. The dam is 1,800 feet long (550m) and 170 feet (52m) high. It was begun in 1921 and took fifteen years to complete, with 700 men continuously employed. Working on the site were a dozen locomotives and twice as many steam cranes. The village population grew to 1,100, and there were many shops such as grocer, hairdresser, butcher, draper, fishmonger and newsagent. There was even a fish and chip shop, as well as a church, school, cinema, concert hall, recreation room, billiards room, writing room and tennis courts. The men were housed in ten hostels and sixty bungalows. Harking back to those wild times, an old farmer said how there used to be a fight every night, and that there hasn't been a good fight in the dale since!

The foundations of the temporary village can still be seen below the dam on the far side, and you can imagine the double-headed trains (with a banker, too) belching forth clouds of steam and smoke as they puffed up the steep incline, bringing materials to the dam site.

By 1937, the shanty town had been removed and the dam — said to be the largest masonry dam in Europe — was ready to hold back over two thousand million gallons of water. The water pipeline to Bradford reappears in Wharfedale, where it crosses the river below Barden Bridge in the familiar castellated structure. The tunnel was dug on four faces, from Scar House, from Wharfedale and from each side of a shaft below Greenhow. The tunnels met up perfectly, being only an inch or so out of line.

(It is worth mentioning that a circuit of Scar House Reservoir makes a fine four mile (6½km) walk, crossing Angram Dam (completed in 1911). On the way is the old farmhouse of Lodge — formerly a lodge of Byland Abbey. In 1728, Maggie Thompson of 'Lodge End' was strongly suspected of the murder of three Scottish pedlars, their headless bodies having been found in the peat on what is now Dead Man's Hill. The account book for Middlesmoor still has the entry: 'three murdered bodies were found buried on Lodge Edge without heads'. There are several old tracks over to Coverdale, the best being the old road that goes between Dead Man's Hill and Little Whernside.)

However, our route now crosses the 600 yard (550m) dam wall of Scar House. (There are toilets at the car park.) Turn right, alongside the reservoir as far as a gate, then double back up the hillside for the return route. The path winds up to a gritstone quarry, from which stone was obtained for construction of the dam (there is another large quarry on the opposite side of the valley on Carle Fell), and up onto Rain Stang.

Here is the home of the grouse, the golden plover, meadow pipit and curlew. Meadow pipits often perch on the walls, but use their song-flight to stake out their territory. The golden plover's evocative piping *klew-ee* is often the first indication of the bird's presence, and a careful search with binoculars may bring it into view, as it stands its ground in the near distance. The curlew returns to the moors in February or March and, as a sign of spring, there are few sounds more welcome than its bubbling song. The curlew is most vociferous after the chicks are hatched.

Along In Moor Lane, the track becomes walled on both sides, and to the right is the valley of Stean Beck with the peak of Meugher behind it. Ahead, a lovely view of Gouthwaite Reservoir appears, as the track gently descends to Middlesmoor.

SELECTED READING

Geology and scenery:
Colin Scrutton (ed), *Yorkshire Rocks and Landscape, A Field Guide* (Yorkshire Geological Society, 1994). Includes itineraries to upper Nidderdale, Brimham, Harlow Carr and Knaresborough.
H C Versey, *Geology and Scenery Round Leeds and Bradford* (Thomas Murby, 1948). Contains itineraries in the Knaresborough and Harrogate districts.
Tony Waltham, *Yorkshire Dales: Limestone Country* (Constable, 1987). Useful if you are thinking of visiting Goyden Pot.

History:
J G Blacker, *The Stone Industry of Nidderdale* (the author, 1993). A small booklet available from the Nidderdale Museum, Pateley Bridge.
Bernard Jennings (ed) *A History of Nidderdale* (Advertiser Press, Huddersfield, 1967). A wonderful piece of research on the dale written by the Pateley Bridge Local History Tutorial Class, under the direction of Professor Bernard Jennings, then of Leeds University.
Arnold Kellett, *Historic Knaresborough* (Smith Settle, 1991). An enthusiastic and scholarly history of the town, beautifully and profusely illustrated.
Malcolm G Neesam, *Exclusively Harrogate* (Smith Settle, 1989). A well-illustrated history of the town and its growth as a spa.
Harry Speight, *Nidderdale, from Nun Monkton to Whernside* (Elliot Stock, 1906). Still a useful text on the history of the dale and its families.

Natural History:
Harrogate and District Naturalists, *Birds of the Harrogate District* (1991), and a series of booklets on the wildlife of Nidderdale, including *Insectivorous Mammals, Small Rodents, Amphibians, Butterflies*, and *Wildlife of the Nidd Gorge*. All are illustrated with black and white photographs, and many have distribution maps of species.
The Nidd Gorge Project: *Bilton Beck Woods and Nature Trail, Nidd Gorge Geological Trail* and *The Conyngham Hall Trail* are a series of useful leaflets produced by Harrogate Borough Council, Department of Technical Services.
H Henzel, R Fitter and J Parslow, *Pocket Guide to Birds of Britain and Europe* (Collins). Collins also do a larger 'Field Guide' and a small and handy 'Gem Guide'.
Franklyn Perring, *RSNC Guide to British Wild Flowers* (Country Life Books, 1984). A useful book for beginners and others; not exhaustive, but it describes 330 of our most familiar wild flowers.

Walking:
J K E Piggin, *Nidderdale Way* (Dalesman, 1983) Ken Piggin has done a great service to walkers in Nidderdale. The fifty-three mile (85km) circuit is well-signposted and waymarked.
Harrogate Borough Council, *The Harrogate and Knaresborough Ringway Footpath*. Available from the Tourist Information Office, Crescent Road, Harrogate.

INDEX

Illustrative references are indicated by *italics*